# CLARENCE DARROW

## and

## the American Literary Tradition

# Clarence Darrow

### and

the American Literary Tradition

*by* ABE C. RAVITZ

Professor of English
Hiram College

THE PRESS OF WESTERN

RESERVE UNIVERSITY

1962

Copyright 1962 by Western Reserve University
Library of Congress Catalogue Card Number 62–17760
Manufactured in the United States of America.

*For*
ESTHER

# CONTENTS

# ACKNOWLEDGMENTS

My deepest appreciation goes to the Library of Congress Manuscript Division for permitting me to examine the Clarence Darrow Papers; to the New York Public Library and to the Chicago Public Library for making available to me rare pamphlet and newspaper material relating to the attorney and his works; to the Hiram College Library and the Hiram College Fund for Research for invaluable help, scholarly and financial.

The author gratefully acknowledges the kindness of Mr. Ernest L. Knuti, attorney of Chicago and executor of the estate of Mrs. Ruby H. Darrow, for permission to quote from the Darrow Papers; and of the following owners of copyrighted material used in this book: Holt, Rinehart, and Winston ("The Culprit," by A. E. Housman), G. P. Putnam's Sons (*The Rhymes of Ironquill*), and Charles Scribner's Sons (*Farmington* and *The Story of My Life* by Clarence Darrow).

I am equally grateful to Mr. Rees Davis, Jr., attorney of Cleveland, and Miss Rose Vormelker, Librarian of the Cleveland *Plain Dealer*, for aid in tracking down Chris Merry details; to Mr. Willis Thornton, Director of the Western Reserve University Press, for his sympathetic pencil; to Mrs. Margaret Clapp, Mrs. David Phillips, and Miss Virginia Waratinsky for research and typing assistance.

# *Prologue*

# WHIRLPOOL

THE mind of Clarence Darrow was a confluence of culture and anarchy. Like a tangled skein of random, undisciplined threads, the knots of his intellect present a challenging series of hooks and twists weaving a chartless design through those socio-intellectual upheavals which during the second half of the nineteenth century disturbed alike the esoteric thinkers and the crossroads philosophers. To deal with an intellectual anomaly, as Darrow assuredly was, necessitates not only studying those sources from which his mutinous genius culled idea and direction, but also isolating for exclusive scrutiny the major influences which made up the literary personality of this unusually talented attorney. Thus, with the logic of a legal brief the task looms clear: dissevering the web of disparate concepts, refining its content in terms of epoch and background, and, at length, linking its significance to the major pattern of American thought. At the very least, then, an *apologia* for Darrow's extensive intellectual indebtedness and a statement of his various mental figurations are in order.

The attention of Clarence Darrow was captured early by the Darwinian thesis and its societal and spiritual consequences. In expounding a social pessimism derived from evolutionary thought, Dr. Max Nordau during the 1890's dissected, with nihilistic bellowings, the innate sickness of a *fin-de-siècle* world. His iconoclastic decimation of contemporary civilization became part and parcel of the ethic adopted by young Darrow. In the writings of Herbert Spencer, too, Darwin's apparent ambassador of philosophy to America, Darrow first perceived the entanglement of science with society and unhappily realized the cold premises of Evolution and their fundamental debasement of man's individual integrity. The religion of Free Thought, implicit in Darwinism, Clarence Darrow also encountered early in his career, and the newspaper productions of Francis Ellingwood Abbot and Eugene Fitch Ware continued to augur for the attorney what was to become a permanent fixture in his philosophical orbit: life offered at best a tolerable and at worst a dreary tomorrow. Yet the formative and maturative years of Darrow's mind also found the attorney whittling and chopping ideas from Tolstoy and Ingersoll, from Emerson and Altgeld. With this imposing backdrop of nineteenth-century titans as collective progenitor, a chronicle which smoothly disentangles individual channels of Darrow's thought becomes a needless and virtually impossible exercise. The lawyer's novels and tales, essays and lectures are literal compendia of the ideas associated with these diverse authorities.

Equally significant in its influence on the mind and art of Clarence Darrow is Puritanism, a heritage ". . . firmly rooted in the American experience" over which it has cast an imposing shadow since the very planting of the Massachusetts Bay Colony. Unaware of the thirty-eight connotations which Charles A. Beard in the *New Republic* (December, 1920) ascribed to this New England complex of socio-theocratic forces, Darrow adopted a view that ranged the so-called "original" Puritanism of the Bay Colony alongside the later Puritanism emerging from the Great Awakening of the late eighteenth century. Evangelical and Fundamentalist derivations, of course, characterized the religious affections of The Awakening, whose trademark of enthusiasm imbued with a new spirit the history of early American theology. As the attorney had found suggested in the principles of Integration and Disintegration elucidated by Herbert Spencer, so each of the socio-theological patterns, the old Puritanism and the new, came to deepen Darrow's artistic reservoir. Indeed, with Evolution and Puritanism as the vital wellsprings of his thought, the flow of ideas issuing from the mind of Clarence Darrow leads to an involved, exciting odyssey along the involuted byways of the American dream and some of its grim historical realities.

Clarence Darrow thought of himself as a creative artist, and for a time early in his career seriously considered forsaking law to pursue the literary Muse. During the 1890's, when this newcomer from the Western Reserve of Ohio was prominent in the machine politics of Chicago and was, at the same time, gaining a national reputation as America's foremost labor lawyer, he lectured and pamphleteered not only on controversial political and social questions of the day (The Boer War, The Irish Problem, Bolshevism) but also on Realism in literature and art and brought out a collection of critical essays, *A Persian Pearl*. When he was retained by William Randolph Hearst to incorporate the Chicago *Evening American*, Darrow, gratis, immediately began contributing a little-known series of tales, *Easy Lessons in Law*, to his employer's newspaper. In the early years of the twentieth century the versatile Darrow published two novels—*Farmington* (1904) and *An Eye for An Eye* (1905)—and came to be regarded by the most eminent of the country's literati as a powerful associate in the contemporary movement to turn American letters toward the road of Realism. William Dean Howells had observed that Darrow's summation in the Kidd Case of 1898 was "as interesting as a novel," and Hamlin Garland at the very height of his powers as novelist and critic labeled Darrow a "poet." Brand Whitlock, soon to become a distinguished American statesman, as well as a highly-respected novelist, based much of his social theory and all of his critical orientation on the principles Clarence Darrow outlined for him. It was, indeed, literary talent-scout Darrow who discovered Whitlock and who brought this rising star to the attention of Howells.

After 1905 Darrow's creative energy was directed toward the courtroom and brought him into some of the most notable trials in the history of American jurisprudence. He managed to devote much attention, nevertheless, to writing both for popular and *avant garde* journals, and during the 'twenties and 'thirties became a prolific essayist who joined H. L. Mencken in his crusade against Boobocracy. A familiar contributor to the numerous insurgent magazines of the day, Darrow also lectured furiously in behalf of those principles of right-mindedness which he felt were being profaned by heresy-hunters intent on unearthing Red subversion and by morals legislators who regarded the Volstead Act as the Eleventh Commandment and Anthony Comstock as a new Moses. Darrow's writings during these times are as intrinsic a part of American social and literary history as the productions stemming from the Mencken-Nathan combine which traumatized many a provincial prude who saw America coming to an end, suffocated by "jelly beans," flappers and their sinful advocates. *The Story of My Life* (1932), Clarence Darrow's autobiography, recounted with happy satisfaction the lawyer's part in the making of America from the troublesome days of the IWW to the turbulent era of the New Deal.

All the time his pen was flashing, now as a creative talisman and now as an explosive weapon, across the scheme of American letters.

Darrow was born in April, 1857, at precisely the time when Herman Melville's "Rabelaisan piece of patchwork," *The Confidence Man*, was irritating critics because of its "irreverent use of Scriptural phrases." The attorney, like Melville, was to become more than a fugitive commentator on the American scene, but unlike Melville, whose achievements are embodied in the historical panorama of mid-nineteenth-century American literary renaissance, the exploits of Clarence Darrow project an image of the contemporaneous. This lawyer of near-legendary proportions, however, was born before Darwin revealed the natural selectionist theories that were to make of him a monumental cultural force; before Lincoln and Douglas took to the stump for their historic, even mythic, debates; before Henry Wadsworth Longfellow gave to an adulatory public his revered schoolroom favorite, "The Courtship of Miles Standish"; and in the same year as the founding of that constant on the rapidly changing scene of American periodical literature, the *Atlantic Monthly*. During the childhood of Clarence Darrow, the intelligentsia looked to the latest emanation from the pen of Spencer, whose *Social Statics; or, The Conditions Essential to Human Happiness* explained the vagaries and perversities of human behavior. Sigmund Freud's *Die Traumdeutung* was nearly half a century away from publication. Darrow's little Western Reserve town, zealous in its Abolitionist stance, reverberated with nineteenth-century opprobriums of "Copperhead" and "Dirt Eater," rather than "Bolshevik" and "Anarchist," brands of the future.

Darrow's past, then, was strongly anchored in deep roots of the nineteenth century, and from the earliest years his surroundings reflected controversy splashed by the broadest, most elemental concepts of right and wrong, bondage and freedom, good and evil; by the bewildering chaos of a stormy and speculative, yet a genteel and gilded, age. As the twentieth century began to unfold, the personality of this "craggy man" came to dominate circles humanitarian and iconoclastic. From the pocket cults of social reform and Perfectionism, however, he emerged at transient, though frequent, moments to assume a place in the humanistic stream of America's literary heritage. The whirl of letters came to suffuse the attorney's creative intellect in much the same way as the theater forever allured Henry James. Clarence Darrow's attempts, achievements, and failures in these areas, his relationships and ties with the American literary grain, his intellectual idols and aesthetic responsibilities contain the seeds of a tale that adds an important new perspective through which to regard one of the most glamorous and controversial heroes of our times.

# Chapter 1

## JEREMIADS

THE tensions of Haymarket still enveloped a nervous, unsettled Chicago when in 1888 Clarence Seward Darrow, fresh from a modest law practice in Ashtabula, Ohio, determined to assail and conquer the big city with his legal talents. Although two years had passed since, as the Chicago *Times* noted, "arch counselors of riot, pillage, incendiarism, and murder" bombed a peaceable labor meeting in the process of being scattered by the police and thus exploded Anarchism with vile prominence across banner headlines, the Chicago of 1888—the town of Cyrus McCormick, George Pullman, and the Beef Trust—remained a seething mass of "despoilers" and "despoiled." When Ignatius Donnelly wryly observed that contemporary society embodied only millionaires and tramps, he overstated dramatically what was apparent to even the most unperceptive traveller through the city to which Clarence Darrow now came. With an absurdly uncomplicated structure, Chicago, its "toilers and idlers," as John R. McMahon, a proletarian fictionist, described the situation, presented in sharply defined positives and negatives the clearest socio-economic antipodes ever manifested in so complex and turbulent a community. To the Elect came wealth, power, religion, and law; to the Reprobate fell poverty, degradation, atheism, and license. Darrow later asserted that the vortex of humanity into which he was hurled constituted "fishers of fish and fishers of each other."

Clarence Darrow had come to a frightened city whose mayor, the Honorable Carter H. Harrison, had recently issued a warning to avoid "gatherings of people in crowds or processions in the streets and public places" as a safeguard against "bad men . . . armed with cowardly missiles, for the purpose of bringing about bloodshed." Prominent citizens had confessed themselves "horrified" over the "inciting utterances" of Cardinal Manning, an English reformist-cleric, who openly proclaimed that "Necessity has no law, and a starving man has a right to his neighbor's bread." These guardians of Chicago's social structure built atop the shambles of gaudy gingerbread and gilded tinsel, found contemporary justification for the obvious inequalities in the class structure by citing the stratification inherent in the unvarying laws of Nature which determined not only the biological phenomena surrounding human behavior but also the economic and political motives and campaigns of life. Conservative Darwinism happily explained with a mathematical certitude the necessary logic behind the "haves" and the "have nots." Darrow found himself immersed in this maelstrom of complacency and panic, where, eschewing from the very first those fashionable ideas to which the respectable (Elect) were expected to subscribe, he, with characteristic defiance, aligned himself with the prophets of what Theodore Roosevelt was later to call "the lunatic fringe"; from these anathemas of polite society he began to nurture and develop that philosophic focus and orientation which he was later to dramatize in his belletristic writing and to popularize in his courtroom oratory.

The ambitious lawyer soon joined the Single-Tax Club where discussions of the Henry George land ethic were often bypassed in favor of harangues on the Boer War and capital punishment. Indeed, at this time Darrow had become a correspondent of Henry Demarest Lloyd, the so-called "Middle-Class Conscience" whose "progressivism [was] a religion as well as a political faith" and who wrote the young lawyer in 1894 that "They [Socialists] are the most intelligent, most energetic, most reliable workers we have." By the middle 1890's Darrow was lecturing not only in behalf of the Boers but also in support of Irish independence:

> . . . the strong, constant, ever futile effort of conservatism, oppression and tyranny [is] to hold back the resistless tide of progress; to restrain that great sea which ever alternately ebbs and flows, but which, through all, is ever rising higher and higher and sweeping away thrones and empires and states, laws and customs and institutions, and slowly widening the liberty of man. (*The Rights and Wrongs of Ireland,* [Chicago, 1895])

At Central Music Hall, the Garrick Theater, the Sunset Club and other forums for public expression, Darrow quickly became exposed to some of the most controversial personalities of the era;

to intellectuals under the influence of the *"fin-de-siècleism"* currently being washed up on American shores from effete European circles; and to iconoclasts whose tendencies toward anarchy and nihilism were being aped over here by so-called professional "Bohemians" looking to escape from strait-jacket conformity into a dreamy Vagabondia attractively painted by two collaborative poets of the mauve decade, Bliss Carman and Richard Hovey:

> . . . Off with the fetters
> That chafe and restrain!
> Off with the chain!
> —Here we are free
> Free as the wind is,
> Free as the sea,
> Free!

The most provocative "Jeremiah of the period," however, was Dr. Max Nordau, whose anointed task seemed to be alerting humanity that ". . . mankind with all its institutions and creations is perishing in the midst of a dying world" and that *fin-de-siècleism* is a "mood" characterized by "the impotent despair of a sick man, who feels himself dying by inches in the midst of an eternally living nature blooming insolently forever." Forecasting the "end of an established order," Nordau lamented as being too swift and formless "emancipation from traditional discipline":

> To the voluptuary this [*fin-de-siècleism*] means unbridled lewdness, the unchaining of the beast in man; to the withered heart of the egoist, disdain of all consideration for his fellowmen, the trampling under foot of all barriers which enclose brutal greed of lucre and lust of pleasure; to the contemner of the world it means the shameless ascendancy of base impulses and motives, which were, if not virtuously suppressed, at least hypocritically hidden; to the believer it means repudiation of dogma, the negation of a super-sensuous world, the descent into flat phenomenalism; to the sensuous nature yearning for aesthetic thrills, it means the vanishing of ideals in art. . . .

Things "totter and plunge" about wildly, while "there is a sound of rending in every tradition, and it is as though the morrow would not link itself with today." Thus Nordau in *Degeneration*, a best-seller in America during 1895, cautioned that revolt must have substance and direction, that fallacies of existence must be rooted out as social cancers. The German doctor's philippics, indeed, even during the 1880's had attracted a considerable following in this country and Louis Schick, a Chicago publisher, had by 1884 brought out two translated editions of Nordau's *The Conventional Lies of Our Civilization*, less arresting but more utilitarian than *Degeneration*, a collection of judgments labeled a "great success" by the Chicago *Tribune*, which further termed the volume a "sensational series of essays." The highly reputable *Literary World* described the Nordau collection as a significant work dealing with "prevalent prejudices; current moral, mental, and social mistakes; deep-rooted literary and scientific errors; being a brilliantly written compound of great truths and clever exaggerations, of earnest enthusiasm and phantastic impossibilities." In Chicago's intellectual circles of the day, then, Nordau was discussed by the discontented, the seekers, and the "Bohemians" as frequently and intensely as the blight and horror of Packingtown and child labor. The physician's agglomeration of nineteenth-century skepticism and his own brand of *fin-de-siècle* iconoclasm led him in the *Conventional Lies* to numerous categorical pronouncements which Clarence Darrow by the turn of the century had adopted and was to champion throughout his career. The Nordau stage of his education toughened the fibers of pessimism in a young lawyer dazzled by the ease and flash of these scattershot, "audacious" essays.

The basic premise behind Nordau's literary ambush became the primary assumption lurking behind the ethic of Clarence Darrow. Stated the doctor on page one of *Conventional Lies:*

> The world of Civilization is an immense hospital ward, the air is filled with groans and lamentations, and every form of suffering is to be seen twisting and turning on the beds.

Upon the dismal world view substantiated by the Hobbesian dialectic that regards man as a wolf to man, justice and morality become subverted by natural science and Social Darwinism. Especially when Dr. Nordau undertook an examination of what was called "the Economic Lie" did he begin to probe a sensitive area of particular concern to the starry-eyed attorney. "At no period in the world's history were the contrasts between rich and poor so decided, so prominent, as at present," stipulated Nordau (*Lies*, p. 194) in complete accord with Ignatius Donnelly's observation and thus gave sound expression to a statement of fact then becoming painfully evident to the Chicago counselor. As the indignant doctor writes concerning "the slavery of the factory employee," who, while conscious of his dignity and "natural rights as a man," is merely "a kind of forlorn post which every disease tries in turn to master," he is no longer flitting as a cherubic iconoclast shooting wooden darts of half-hearted reformism but now assumes the stature of a tortured social commentator with righteous ire directed at the "band of robbers" for which "the whole community toils." The conspicuous consumption of robber barons leads Nordau to attack without mercy all articles of luxury with which the rich showered themselves:

> I do not hesitate then to declare that no human being has the right to demand the gratification of his whims, as long as the actual necessities of others are unsatisfied, to employ workmen in the production of fireworks . . . as long as others are famishing . . . to condemn the factory operatives to fourteen hours a day of slavish toil, so that the price of velvet may be low enough for him [the robber baron] to clothe himself in the material the most pleasing to his esthetic taste. (*Lies*, p. 249).

The immoral physical privation inflicted upon the day laborer would make of the city, in a matter of time, "an enormous cemetery, without a single living being within its walls, if it were not for the fact that there is a constant influx of people from the country to fill up the ranks left vacant by death." Indeed, the worker "is the sole living being in the universe who spends the greater part of his lifetime in work contrary to nature, merely to keep himself alive"; such a pitiable inmate of "dreary factory walls," finds "no opportunity to enjoy the mere privilege of living." The pose of the scoffing cynic was dropped by Nordau as he obviously stumbled upon a truth that usurped an ethical prominence in the thesis he was promulgating, and in his section on the Economic Lie, he formulated a series of axioms that became the very basis for the hypotheses developed by Clarence Darrow in his tales and novels of bio-economic warfare.

Nordau terminated his book with a "Closing Harmony," a series of ambiguities dealing with "Progress and enlightenment" and "the solidarity of humanity." The "catechism" of the universe, "Nature's morality," contains an "indestructible principle" that "forms an elementary constituent of the human consciousness": the "immutable principle of human fellowship." Through this impelling force, the biological struggle for existence will become by degrees milder and at length diminish to a negligible phenomenon: "The civilization of today whose characteristics are pessimism, lying, and selfish egotism, [will be] followed by a civilization of truth, love of one's neighbor and cheerfulness." Thus the great good society is in the future, and the anodyne prescribed by Dr. Nordau resembles the panacea that Clarence Darrow was, during the same era, outlining for his audiences:

> More than all things else it [civilization] means the cultivation of a broad, charitable, humane spirit that makes man feel a closer kinship to his fellow man. . . . The century is closing; the old is dying; the new, let us hope, is coming.

Max Nordau was whipped into an intellectual frenzy by the evident paradoxes of Darwinism—the ruthless struggle toward an evolutionary perfection; the ultimate achievement of a cosmic optimism only after plodding through the painful morass of weary pessimism. Clarence Darrow's iconoclasm sprang from a similar emotional fountainhead: the logical view of Conservative Darwinism in making universally applicable survival of the fittest and the distressing realization that brute fatalism was anathema to concepts of romantic individualism and its belief that man must emerge as a product of his own consciousness, undergoing his pragmatic confrontation of life as being an experience rather than a battleground. With only shimmering, elusive abstractions that reveal no portion of a unified philosophy, Nordau accentuated for Darrow and the *zeitgeist* a genesis of despair on which to base the problems of the new century. It was Herbert Spencer, however, who finally united for Darrow and other "tyros in philosophy" everything in nature, so Richard Hofstadter asserts, "from protozoa to politics." [1]

The extent to which Clarence Darrow's ultimate intellectual orientation depended on the philosophy of Herbert Spencer was sharply illustrated by Will Durant's observation in 1928:

---

[1] *Social Darwinism in American Thought* (Boston, 1955), pp. 31–32.

Mr. Darrow, of course, is still living in the age of Herbert Spencer: his philosophy and science have not, perhaps, come down from that mid-Victorian age. He would think as Spencer did of the mind as simply a readjustment to external things, of education as an adjustment of the individual to the environment.[2]

Like the English popularizer of Darwinism, Darrow, avoiding the reconciliation of the scientific (evolutionary) and theological (fundamentalist) accounts of genesis, thus clothed his resolution of the dilemma in the 1920's:

Herbert Spencer in his "First Principles" has shown how impossible it is to find the ultimate explanation. . . . I feel, with Herbert Spencer, that whether the universe had an origin—and if it had—what the origin is will never be known by man.

Indeed, the imposing intellect of Spencer, "metaphysician of the homemade intellectual, and . . . prophet of the cracker-barrel agnostic," proved highly attractive during the 'eighties and 'nineties to "village agnostics . . . scientists, many theologians, and most captains of industry." One cannot, furthermore, minimize Spencer's powerful impact on the intellectuals of the time, for Professor John Fiske, nineteenth-century America's most respected and prolific historian, extolled "the endlessly rich and suggestive thoughts which he has thrown out in such profusion by the wayside all along the course of [his] great philosophical enterprise." Rhapsodically, Fiske went on to avow that Spencer's "is work of the caliber of that which Aristotle and Newton did."[3] The Synthetic Philosophy of Spencer, clearly, was found not only in vest pockets of cranks, skeptics and visionaries but also in drawing rooms, academic convocations, and houses of worship.

Creating a system of such wide appeal, Spencer impressed disciples with his vast knowledge in all areas of human understanding. He took upon himself the monumental task of codifying into a single comprehensive unity all the recent theories of Darwin, Lyell,

[2] *Are We Machines: Is Life Mechanical or Is It Something Else?* (Haldeman-Julius pamphlet, 1928), p. 50. A Durant-Darrow debate.

[3] "Herbert Spencer's Service to Religion," *Essays Historical and Literary* II (New York, 1902), 230. Text of an address delivered November 9, 1882.

and Lamarck; the physical experimentations of Helmholtz, Kelvin, and Mayer; the economics of Malthus and the sociology of Comte. In the death struggle between Science and Religion, Evolution and Faith, the compendiums of Herbert Spencer were aimed at uplifting the spirit from the calm, casual resignation many a beleaguered churchman had adopted, at the same time revealing to the scientist the primacy of his place in this mysterious world order. Lay philosophers everywhere found in Spencer intellectual fodder enabling them to harmonize or dissociate right reason and unshakable faith. In this aura of rational and spiritual exploration, Clarence Darrow became an ardent Spencerian, with *First Principles* and *Social Statics* literally coming to be regarded by the attorney as divine pronouncements on the human situation. "Philosophy," Spencer wrote, "is completely unified knowledge," and through reading his works Darrow came to feel that he had seen formulated and centralized the manifold and chaotic realities of existence that his own contact with life had evoked.

*First Principles*, in its fourth edition by 1880, has Spencer, amid glamorous, eye-catching phrases—"The Indestructibility of Matter," "The Continuity of Motion," "The Persistence of Force," "The Instability of the Homogeneous," "Equilibration," "Dissolution"—set forth his reflections, physical and metaphysical, concerning the organic and the super-organic (Language, Art, Science, and Literature) constituency of the universe. Basically, through Spencer's scientific headlines one can trace his theory as deduced by the nineteenth-century intellectually curious layman. Matter and Motion, driven to constant flux by the Persistence of Force, easily change "any finite homogeneous aggregate" into a stabilized heterogeneity through processes labeled Evolution (progressive metamorphosis from lowest forms of life to highest organisms) and Dissolution (the complement of Evolution that undoes what Evolution has done). Decay must follow the apex of attainment; death and disintegration occur when the evolutionary limits are reached. The antithetical concepts of Spirit and Matter are "to be regarded as but a sign of the Unknown Reality which underlies both."

The evolutionary cycle was made so clear by Spencer that its application beyond the boundaries of biology was facile and apparent. "All things are growing or decaying," he observed, "accumulating matter or wearing away, integrating or disintegrating."

Everywhere there are processes of life in antagonism, "gaining now a temporary and now a more or less permanent triumph the one over the other." These underlying principles on which he based his entire scheme, Spencer thus defined:

> Evolution under its simplest and most general aspect is the integration of matter and concomitant dissipation of motion; while dissolution is the absorption of motion and concomitant disintegration of matter.

The limits of Evolution bring humanity to Equilibrium, a state of balance and stability (equilibrium) for the individual organism or the society. Each society observes this principle "in the continuous adjustment of its population to its means of subsistence." Equilibration is also seen, Spencer notes, in the establishment of governments which must "fall into harmony with the desires of the people." Antagonistic forces within the Evolutionary—Dissolutionary cycle, then, become evident in the conflicts between Conservatism, "which stands for the restraints of society over the individual," and Reform, "which stands for the liberty of the individual against society." Hence the natural resistance man develops against all restraint imposed by society takes the form of man himself endeavoring to limit "the sphere of action" of other individuals. The Evolutionism that Darrow found so lucidly expressed in Spencer, a system designed, so the Englishman asserted, to establish "the greatest perfection and the most complete happiness," was the brutish drive which Nordau's vehement naturalism had outlined for the attorney as the unscrupulous life force intent on perfection at the expense of less-endowed innocents. While the economics of such a theory was attractive to Combines of the era, Darrow wondered at the deplorable loss of beauty and utility in the dissolution of the less-endowed. Nathaniel Hawthorne in 1843 had allegorized a solemn warning against such violation of humanity by his tale of "The Birthmark," where Aylmer, a scientist, disturbed at his wife Georgiana's single imperfection—a crimson mark, barely distinguishable, in the center of her left cheek—determines to eradicate the blemish through his science. The result:

> As the last crimson tint of the birthmark—that sole token of human imperfection—faded from her cheek, the parting breath of the now perfect woman passed into the atmosphere,

and her soul, lingering a moment near her husband took its heavenward flight.

Hawthorne's lesson is clear:

> Thus ever does the gross fatality of earth exult in its invariable triumph over the immortal essence which, in this dim sphere of half development, demands the completeness of a higher state.

While the tale reveals that the application of scientific perfectionism to the physical mainstream of human experience is uncharitable, its major thesis resounds with the fundamental integrity of the human personality which is a sacred entity transcending both hostile Nature and scientific theory. Clarence Darrow, as romantic an individualist as Nathaniel Hawthorne, was always beseiged by this basic conflict between the now and the utopian. He might reluctantly concur with Herbert Spencer, yet have little sympathy for those theories which intellectual honesty urged him to maintain.

Spencer's thoughts toward a perfectionist commonwealth were expounded for Darrow in *Social Statics*, a basic sociological text of the day. Spencer confessed a "cruelty" inherent in the "stern discipline" of evolution, but explained that barbarity existed to be "very kind":

> That state of universal warfare maintained throughout the lower creation, to the great perplexity of many worthy people, is at bottom the most merciful provision which the circumstances admit of. It is much better that the ruminant animal, when deprived by age of the vigour which made its existence a pleasure, should be killed by some beast of prey, than it should linger out a life made painful by infirmities, and eventually die of starvation. By the destruction of all such, not only is existence ended before it becomes burdensome, but room made for a younger generation capable of the fullest enjoyment; and, moreover, happiness is derived for a tribe of predatory creatures.

This code of existence "is pitiless in the working out of good," for "higher creation" ("civilization") is the "last stage of its accomplishment," and everything is oriented toward the inevitable progress along the road to an abstract ideal of Perfection. Existing humanity, therefore, is subject to that "beneficent, though severe, discipline" which revolves about "the mercy of severity." Spencer postulates:

> The poverty of the incapable, the distresses that come upon the imprudent, the starvation of the idle, and those shoulderings aside of the weak by the strong, which leave so many "in shallows and in miseries," are the decrees of a large, far-seeing benevolence.

No social evils, Spencer continues, can be rectified by reform, for there is no "removable cause." "Spurious philanthropists," in order to "prevent present misery, would entail greater misery on future generations," by attempting to referee the social and economic struggle for existence. Misery and suffering, nevertheless, are necessary properties in the eventual eradication of all imperfection. Mankind must accept the unpalatable conclusion that

> Humanity is being pressed against the inexorable necessities of its new position—in being moulded into harmony with them, and has to bear the resulting unhappiness as best it can. The process *must* be undergone, and the sufferings *must* be endured. No power on earth, no cunningly devised laws of statesmen, no world-rectifying schemes of the humane, no communist panaceas, no reforms that man ever did broach or ever will broach, can diminish them one jot.

The philanthropist can, perhaps, prevent the "intensification" of the process at a given moment in time, but, generally, "justice aggravates" the condition and prolongs the agony of ultimate and certain doom. The picture, to say the least, is not a pretty one, and staring at Darrow from the pages of Spencer's explicit prose was the hopelessness of humanitarian effort juxtaposed with gloomy portents of determinism. The Chicago attorney appreciated, however, the theological stance taken by the Englishman; that is, behind the concepts of Spirit and Matter—behind the entire motivational structures embodied by the Darwinism he was endeavoring to popularize—lay an "Unknown Reality." By this calculated ambiguity, Spencer did not displease the theologians, nor did he seriously disturb the scientists or alienate the "free-thinkers" from subscribing to his philosophy. Darrow, indeed, found justification for his agnosticism in Spencer's writings.

On the other hand, Clarence Darrow could not align his ethic with the grim carnage constantly going on about him—a socio-biological struggle incapable of alleviation on a permanent basis. His outlook refused to permit turning his back on the under-privileged, claiming as basis for rationale their inexorable doom—even a fortuitous demise leading to final harmony and Perfection. Spencer, nevertheless, served definite purpose in the lubrication of Clarence Darrow's intellectual processes. The Englishman acquainted Darrow with a "scientific" explication, in commonplace raiment, of the perpetual crisis faced by fragile man living under immutable laws of fate and destiny. Biological and economic determinism symbolized his thesis as pointedly as theological politics characterized the legal setup of the Massachusetts Bay Colony during the 1630's. The Spencerian presentation, too, stimulated Darrow's romantic individualism by lashing out mercilessly at humanitarian tendencies in general, particularly emphasizing the futility of being a meddler with the fixed principles of the universe. Clarence Darrow could never stack the odds against humanity in so prohibitive a manner.

The intellectual backgrounds of Clarence Darrow were not limited to the *fin-de-siècle* ambuscades of Nordau or the Darwinist fusillades of Spencer, for the attorney's father, Amirus Darrow, village agnostic of Kinsman, Ohio, early indoctrinated his son with a "pragmatic, humanistic theism" which was then unearthing numerous adherents: Free Religion. While Darrow's "infidel" father, in true rationalist fashion, looked to Nature as revelation of deity, his real "Bible" was *The Index*, a weekly free-thought newspaper published from 1870 to 1886, first in Toledo and then in Boston. Edited by Francis Ellingwood Abbot (till 1880) and boasting as its contributors some of the most eminent intellects of nineteenth-century America, *The Index* was more than a farmer's theological almanac. The philosophical viewpoint associated with this newspaper grew out of the spiritual rejuvenation of New England that had been initiated in 1836 when Emerson's essay on *Nature* ignited the imaginations of firebrands and seekers and brought to Lyceum platforms and pulpits the concept of Transcendentalism, whose fervid Ideal spirit imbued American scholars with a dedication to intellectual positivism and spiritual perfectionism. Zealously optimistic and militantly liberal in its devotion to "progress," this organ of the Free Religious Association advertised Ingersoll's "great oration" (*The Gods*), reported Woman Suffrage Conventions, and printed "irreverent" verses:

> Here lies Johnny Kunkapod
> Have mercy on him gracious God,
> As he would on you if he was God,
> And you were Johnny Kunkapod.

*The Index*, furthermore, presented not mere mental stimulation for rustic nonbelievers but substantial declamations from top minds of the day; thus, Thomas Wentworth Higginson on "The Character of Buddha"; Octavius Brooks Frothingham on "Three Short Studies of Christianity"; Samuel Longfellow (the poet's brother) on "The Transformation of Piety"; John Weiss (biographer of Theodore Parker) on "Religion as a Sentiment." Poems by Bryant ("Green River"), Lowell ("The Ancient Faith"), Whittier ("The Poem of Humanity"), and Emma Lazarus ("Outside the Church") appeared in *The Index*, along with selections from the standard anthology pieces of Burns, Milton, and Wordsworth; subscribers to Abbot's journal were kept in close contact with the private utterances and public appearances of James Freeman Clarke, Bronson Alcott, Wendell Phillips, and Emerson. At last the Chicago *Tribune* in April, 1872, took strong notice of the impious effects Abbot's new theology was having on mankind:

### MR. DARWIN AND FREE RELIGION

Mr. Darwin, the great Natural Selectionist, has at last selected a creed, and, as a matter of purely local pride, it may be said that he has selected a Western creed; narrowing it down, an Ohio creed; the creed of Mr. Abbot of Toledo, who claims to have brought the truest science and the truest religion into harmony. . . . Mr. Abbot . . . believes Mr. Darwin's Natural Selection theories to be true science and . . . Mr. Darwin believes Mr. Abbot's creed to be true religion. With Mr. Darwin's theories the world is tolerably familiar. . . . . . The effects of Free Religion are to make liberty supreme in all forms of government, science supreme in all forms of belief, morality supreme in all forms of conduct, benevolence supreme in all forms of social relations. It brings the Church, which embodies Christianity, to the level of all other institutions, the Bible to the level of all other books, Christ to the level of all other men, and elevates the

individual, by means of his individual consciousness, above
them all, to progress to his theoretical perfection. . . . Mr.
Abbot's Free Religion is no religion at all, but rather a . . .
set of theories, based on a combination of morality and science; or more strictly speaking, morality governed by science.
There is no hereafter in Mr. Abbot's religious scheme, any
more than there is in Mr. Darwin's scientific scheme; and if,
in accepting Free Religion, Mr. Darwin means to have it
understood that this is the result of his theory of selection as
applied to religion, he will raise a storm about his ears fiercer
than anything he has yet experienced.

The sentiments of *The Index* and its staff became the truths by
which Clarence Darrow was brought up, but the occasional stories
and "masterly" editorials by Francis Ellingwood Abbot, "organizer
and philosopher" of Free Religion in America, illustrated for
Amirus Darrow and his son a social gospel to which both Kinsman
free-thinkers swore eternal allegiance.

The Prospectus of *The Index*, appearing in the first issue (January 1, 1870) embodied a manifesto subservient only to "Truth and
Fact" and announced a new journal of "radical religion" which
desired

> . . . to increase pure and genuine Religion in the world—to
> develop a nobler spirit and higher purpose both in society
> and the individual. It will aim at the same time, to increase
> FREEDOM in the world—to destroy every species of spirit-
> ual slavery, to expose every form of superstition, to encourage
> independence of thought and action in all matters that con-
> cern belief, character or conduct. . . . Without limiting it-
> self to any of the great reformatory movements of the time, it
> proposes to work for them all in the most efficient way, by
> fostering the *spirit of reform*, and by uprooting every con-
> servative prejudice by which reform is checked. . . . It
> will . . . rest solely on the authority of right reason and
> good conscience. It will trust no revelation but that of univer-
> sal human faculties. It will accept every certified result of
> science, philosophy, and historical criticism, asking no ques-
> tion what it proves. Briefly, it will seek the truth and work
> for humanity, believing that man, who makes all institutions,
> can re-make or un-make them as well. . . .

To the inexperienced student of American social thought, here was
as forcible a declaration of intellectual independence as Emerson's

"The American Scholar," for the rational approach to the dilemma of living and believing resounds with irrefutable logic in each line. Abbot actually thought of Free Religion as an escape from the wave of agnosticism which overwhelmed post-Civil War America, but his "Religion of Humanity" eventually became reduced to a brand of muscular atheism altogether socially minded, negating theology completely and concentrating on "here and now" advocacy of the doctrines of progress and perfection. While Clarence Darrow later developed heavy seizures of explosive agnosticism, his philosophical position on theology derived from the dreamy, visionary side of a personality inherited, as far as personality can be inherited, from his father and from Francis Ellingwood Abbot's persuasive editorializing on a plateau that simultaneously overlooked and joined the mundane material statics of day-to-day existence.

The Transcendentalist overtones in Abbot's newspaper contributions derived mainly from the Emersonian doctrine of the World Soul, particularly that segment of the Over-Soul identified as Love. The Toledo Free-Thought leader wrote on "Friendship":

> Is there no profound oneness between Man and Nature, no deep root of unity beneath their evident disparities, no universal life that throbs equally in the ebbings and flowings of cosmical phenomena and the measured systole and diastole of the human heart?

This mystical Oneness, contact with which uplifts the human spirit into becoming a "transparent eyeball" passively accepting the revelations of an Almighty, brings to the abstraction of Friendship another level of expression, a cult of love between man and man; an aesthetic relationship between man and Nature that is at once realistic and symbolic: "Nature is the symbol of spirit," the sage of Concord himself had once observed. In attempting to ascribe to Transcendentalism a practical code for living, Abbot in 1872 wrote on "Organization":

> Organization . . . is the self-expression of living force, the result and proof of vitality. . . . The plant is a composite being; so is humanity. The most profoundly philosophical view of human society is that which makes the race an *organism*. Pure individualism is the crudest type of human existence.

Emerson had noted in his *Journal* "Now and then a man exquisitely made can and must live alone; but coop up most men, and you undo them." Thus the unity of the social schema is the inviolable One from which nonconformity can blossom; and the systems of Emerson and Abbot admitted, even encouraged, easy circulation of social deviates. Free Religion attracted the theologically disinherited and solicited participation in the movement of any and all "illegitimate" creeds; toward this broad principle of toleration Emerson himself, as a youth of twenty-three, had made one of his most significant journal entries:

> A new event is added to the quiet history of my life. I have connected myself by friendship to a man [Achille Murat] who with as ardent a love of truth as that which animates me, with a mind surpassing mine in the variety of its research, and sharpened and strengthened to an energy for *action* to which I have no pretension . . .—is, yet, that which I have ever supposed only a creature of the imagination—a consistent Atheist, and a disbeliever in the existence, and, of course, in the immortality of the soul. My faith in these points is strong and I trust, as I live, indestructible. Meantime I love and honour this intrepid doubter. His soul is noble, and his virtue, as the virtue of a Sadducee must always be, is sublime.

The divinity of man himself was, in the long run, Emerson's singular consideration, and Francis Abbot took the core of workable Transcendentalism, fusing this ethic with the most inspirational elements of man's mystic faith in the World Soul, to provoke readers into renouncing the narrow strait of sectarianism for the broad platform of Free Religion.

*The Index,* believing in political action as part of its metaphysic, publicized Abbot's strong essay on "Radicalism and Conservatism" wherein the author set forth a credo for all free-thinkers who felt that Perfection, necessarily in realms of the purely evolutionary, might be too long in coming:

> The pith and marrow of genuine Radicalism is *Faith in Human Nature and Human Progress, Faith in Man as by the very law of his being developing upwards and not downwards.* So far as the *race* is concerned, it holds that every age is an advance, an improvement on the age preceding; that,

viewed in large segments, man's Present is better than his past and worse than his Future. His origin must have been mean; his destination must be sublime. . . . Radicalism holds that no life is wasted, no soul flung into the arena of existence to be trampled under the heel of an angry God.

By 1872 to flay Calvinism was standard practice of liberal clergy-men who had for some years been preaching of the "New Heaven and the New Earth," Edens devoid of Puritanism; but Abbot went on to buffet this spectre as "the pith and marrow of Conservatism," standing for "*Distrust of Human Nature* [and] *Negation of* Human *Progress.* [*sic*]" The article continued to score this socio-political fallacy:

If left to themselves [conservatives believe] mankind would rush into anarchy and ruin; they need, therefore, to be held in check and submission by means of established institutions in Church and State. . . . Mankind is a fierce brute by nature. . . . To trust men to the guidance of their own natural in-stincts, reason, and conscience . . . is nothing but folly; their tendency is to destruction, not perfection.

It is here that Abbot parted company with Emerson, who saw in "American radicalism" a "destructive and aimless" force and in Conservatism, "able and cultivated," a group "defensive of prop-erty." Wary of reformers, Emerson felt they were afflicted by "incipient insanity," for the real world of divided loyalties, as he suggested in his poem "Days," trooped in oriental procession through his Concord garden while chanting a transcendental hymn of little practical use to abolitionists or other social "utilitarians." For Darrow, Francis Ellingwood Abbot presented the cogent view of man as "Radical"; indeed, it is probable that the pages of *The Index* first brought the moral concern of "Capital Punishment" to the notice of the Kinsman student. In March, 1870, Abbot noted that

Conrad Meier, the convicted and condemned murderer whose execution was appointed to take place in this city on Dec. 8, has just "broke jail" and fled for his life to parts unknown. I am glad of it . . . The great *faith in man* which lies at the root of American civilization and is the grand inspiration of Free Religion, begins already to teach the inviolability of hu-

man life, and to throw a sacred protection even over those
who have themselves dared to violate it. . . . Capital Punishment cannot be for a moment justified to an enlightened
conscience. . . .

Thus open anarchy was part of the literary fare circulated each
week among American free-thinkers, who gradually became sus-
pected of sinister partisan conspiracies against the law of the land.
In later years Clarence Darrow, amused by his "blacklist" at the
hands of the D. A. R., was to many loyal citizens a living manifestation of subversiveness.

The young Buckeye as a matter of course soon became familiar
with another Middle West free-thought purveyor, Eugene Fitch
Ware (1841–1911), Kansas lawyer, poet, and legislator whose
pseudonym, "Ironquill," was a familiar signature to readers of
Topeka newspapers. The cracker-barrel homeyness of the sprawl-
ing frontier was the poetic trademark of Ware, though his
work avoided reliance on a dialect of "Pike County" and on the
backwoods philosophizing of a noble savage like Natty Bumppo.
Actually the free-thought atheism in the *Rhymes of Ironquill*
(eleven editions by 1902!) complemented the polemics Abbot was
issuing from his press in Toledo. Ware's popularity began in the
1870's when his "irreligious" verse "The Washerwoman's Song"
appeared in a newspaper and "shocked orthodox Kansas church-
goers" with its "doubt as to the authenticity of the literal Christian
faith of the catechism":

> In a very humble cot,
>     In a rather quiet spot
> In the suds and in the soap
>     Worked a woman full of hope;
> Working, singing all alone,
>     In a sort of undertone:
> "With the Savior for a friend,
>     He will keep me to the end." ·
>
>             ·  ·  ·  ·
> It's a song I do not sing,
>     For I scarce believe a thing
> Of the stories that are told
>     Of the miracles of old;
> But I know that her belief

> Is the anodyne of grief
> And will always be a friend
> That will keep her to the end.
>
> . . . .
>
> Human hopes and human creeds
> Have their root in human needs
> And I should not wish to strip
> From that washerwoman's lip
> Any song that she can sing,
> Any hopes that songs can bring;
> For the woman has a friend
> Who will keep her to the end.

The poem "over night became famous," so William Allen White records, and established for "Ironquill" a national reputation as "an infidel" violently "skeptical as to most . . . theological schemes. . . ." [4] Ware's simple espousal of Free Religion appealed to Clarence Darrow, who on two occasions—once in an off-the-cuff birthday speech and once when speaking in his own defense before a jury—quoted the Kansan's verse, "Whist":

> Hour after hour the cards were fairly shuffled,
> And fairly dealt, but still I got no hand;
> The morning came, and with a mind unruffled
> I only said, "I do not understand."
>
> Life is a game of whist. From unseen sources
> The cards are shuffled and the hands are dealt;
> Blind are our efforts to control the forces
> That, though unseen, are no less strongly felt.
>
> I do not like the way the cards are shuffled,
> But yet I like the game and want to play;
> And through the long, long night will I, unruffled,
> Play what I get until the break of day.

Applying the "common sense" formula to measure theological validity, Ware presented for Darrow a series of rhymed propositions circumscribing a world view perhaps best summarized by the poet when he wrote in a letter to William E. Connelley, September 14, 1909: "The old earth is only a penal colony, a sort of county jail for the universe." Indeed, the *modus vivendi* of free-

[4] *The Rhymes of Ironquill*, "Foreword," (New York, 1939), p. xvi.

thinking "Ironquill" coincided with the system Clarence Darrow was at the moment formulating; the "Moods" of Eugene Ware communicated with journalese excitement crossroads agnosticism in its most powerful form:

> Of what hope hangs upon
> We can no insight get;
> Blindly fate leads us on,
> Storming life's parapet.
> That which our course impels
> Naught of the future tells.
> ("The Child of Fate")

Away with the flimsy idea that life with a past is attended;
There's Now—only Now, and no Past—there's never a past;
  it has ended.
Away with its obsolete story, and all of its yesterday sorrow;
There's only today, almost gone, and in front of today stands
  tomorrow.

> ("The Now")

> But never have I seen in earth or air,
> A method or a principle. I scan
> An unplanned chaos, shaping here and there
> The greatness and the littleness of man.
> ("Chaos")

Like Clarence Darrow, Eugene Fitch Ware was, according to Charles S. Gleed, "a wholly unconventional lawyer" whose "methods in any given case were more apt to be unprecedented than otherwise." [5] Like Darrow, Ware in the 1890's strongly promulgated the cult of Spencer, writing *The Autobiography of Ithuriel—A Chapter in Psychology* in which he explained for laymen the concept of "Disintegration":

All nature is in a war of competition, and in this great rivalry, when the armies of one are destroyed, its race-atoms, like janizaries, enter into the service of another and keep the discord fervent. The destruction of a race of plants or animals brings about a disintegration of the entire organism down to the very ion. . . . Hence it is that molecules and corpuscles, families and clans, are crumbling and re-forming, combining

[5] *Collections of the Kansas State Historical Society* (1913–1914), p. 39.

and re-combining ever and ever and ever. And out of it all comes an experience, a progress, and an uplift.

The scientific and theological thought patterns motivating Eugene Fitch Ware were the ones most alluring to Clarence Darrow. Ironquill's amply circulated newspaper verses reduced for popular audiences the Free Religion then advocated by the more esoteric writers in the circle of Francis Ellingwood Abbot. Ware, indeed, was a finished product of the Midwest literary free-thinker of the late nineteenth century: robust, though undisciplined, in artistry, liberal in philosophy (Populism and Henry George were the political "bandwagons") and earnest in his quest for spiritual truth: "I must grope and continue to grope." He vowed to "take [his] chances" in the warfare of life, "*ignorant*—unawed."

What finally evolved in the system of Clarence Darrow, exposed to the comparatively sophisticated rationale of the Abbot School and the sub-literary crudity of Ware, was this: Abbot's tendency toward radicalism had been achieved by deriving from Emersonian Transcendentalism those aspects which could be put immediately to practical use in propelling mankind, ahead of Evolutionary schedule, to Perfection. Ware, on the other hand, embroidered drawing-room fatalism, not without sentiment, into a wispy, mysterious predestination devoid of theological alternatives in appealing to romantic speculators on the undeniable ignorance and smallness of man in the universal scope. Darrow's creative aesthetic came to possess potent elements of radical perfectionism as well as sentimental epicureanism. The total impact of free-thought on the attorney was channeled into matters ethical and aesthetic. Theology itself became to Clarence Darrow a substance of negative value utilized for dramatic literary effect (the unequal battle between God and Man) and social paradox (benevolent God condoning human poverty).

Clarence Darrow, hurled into this intellectual matrix fused from *fin-de-siè[cl]eism*, Darwinism, and Free Thought, recognized three clearly-charted literary streams attracting young writers of the day. The most alluring tributary of late nineteenth-century American letters flowed through an aesthetic backwash of the genteel tradition and prospered in airy realms of Romance. Articulately defended and successfully advanced by F. Marion Crawford, E. P.

Roe, Lew Wallace and a coterie of lesser scribblers in fiction, "the old novel," as Darrow termed the popular literary fashion, held little appeal for him. Its hopelessly circumscribed aesthetic he repudiated in "Realism in Literature and Art" (1893):

> The old novel . . . to which the world so fondly clings, had no idea of relation or perspective. It had a hero and a heroine . . . The revolutions of the planets were less important than their love. War, shipwreck and conflagration, all conspired to produce the climax of the scene, and the whole world stood still until the lovers' hearts and hands were joined. Wide oceans, burning deserts, arctic seas, impassable jungles, irate fathers, and even designing mothers, were helpless against the decree that fate had made, and when all the barriers were passed and love had triumphed over impossibilities, the tale was done; through the rest of life nothing of interest could occur. Sometimes in the progress of the story, if the complications were too great, a thunderbolt or an earthquake was introduced to destroy the villain and help on the match.

In this savage account of the stereotyped plot which romances of the Gilded Age brought to the "young American girl," Darrow deliberately cut himself off from the most financially rewarding area of the literary market place. Nor was the young Midwesterner enchanted by the literature of Negativism which had begun its brief, strong vogue at this time. A product of French symbolist writers who had disengaged themselves from the human situation, who had decided to "spit upon the mob," and who retreated into a semi-private universe inhabited by initiates to "art for art's sake" only, this posture in *fin-de-siècle* America took the turn to effete cynicism. Edgar Saltus, the leading fictionist of this group (James G. Huneker was its aesthetician), was regarded as "the prose laureate of pessimism"; he established his bleak reputation as a demonic, "Nay-saying" genius in *The Anatomy of Negation* (nonfiction, 1886):

> Nature, who is unconscious in her immortality, entrancing in her beauty, savage in her cruelty, imperial in her prodigality, and appalling in her convulsions, is not only deaf, but dumb. There is no answer to any appeal. The best we can do, the best that has ever been done, is to recognize the implacability of the laws that rule the universe, and contemplate as calmly

as we can the nothingness from which we are come and into which we shall all disappear.

Clarence Darrow agreed basically with the Saltus view, for the lawyer always thought of himself as a "pessimist." The disenchantments of Saltus, however, emanated from disillusion with the agony he perceived "uncoiling" itself, as he put it, in the "countless maladies" of life which man was powerless to cure. Darrow's negations, on the other hand, were moved by a moral commitment to humanity despite the painful realization that the path leading upward to Perfection was strewn with the mutilated.

The lawyer, about to ascend Parnassus, could not look to the escapism of Romance or to the negativism of contemporary cynics. His orientation adhered to the very mainstream of the American conscience which predicated an existing lifeline between the artist and humanity, a bond that illuminated retreat from mankind as ritual in establishing an ethos for communication between the writer and his world. Thoreau in *Walden* symbolized what he felt was this basic lifeline of responsibility:

> The Fitchburg Railroad touches the pond about a hundred rods south of where I dwell. I usually go to the village along its causeway, and am, as it were, related to society by this link. The men on the freight trains, who go over the whole length of the road, bow to me as to an old acquaintance, they pass me so often, and apparently they take me for an employee; and so I am. I too would fain be a track-repairer somewhere in the orbit of the earth.

The "social threads" by which mankind weaves a necessary "web of relations" held for Emerson also the dictum that individuals, in their quest for perfection, hope to become "no longer strangers and pilgrims in a traditionary globe"; and Nathaniel Hawthorne described man's "universal throb" as a "magnetic chain" possessing a sacrosanct, mystical force whose violation results in the Unpardonable Sin. Indeed, the moral commitment to society was so potent a tenet in the philosophical scheme of Hawthorne that his character Wakefield, who as a joke left his home for a few days, was tragically victimized by this humorous escapade and became "the Outcast of the Universe." The self-annihilation of Hawthorne's Ethan Brand resulted from his casting off the "brotherhood" of man and trampling its "great heart" beneath his feet. Father Mapple, the sailor-priest of New Bedford whose sermon in *Moby-Dick* charted the spiritual voyage of the *Pequod* and its crew, maintained a rope ladder leading to and from his pulpit; his lifeline, like Thoreau's railroad bed, was a visible concretion that "signified his spiritual withdrawal . . . from all outward worldly ties" and at the same time revealed his prime connection with them. Even arrogant Ahab recognized the misfortune of man's necessary reliance on man as he watched the ship's carpenter fashion his peg leg:

> Here I am, proud as a Greek god, and yet standing debtor to this blockhead for a bone to stand on. Cursed be that mortal inter-indebtedness which will not do away with ledgers. I would be free as air; but I'm down in the whole world's books.

A Doctrine of Complicity with similar implications was being preached in another area of the social contract during the 1880's by Darrow's friend William Dean Howells, who advanced in *The Minister's Charge* the thesis that individual sin stems directly from the social sin, that the causative factors in any ethical or moral aberration emanate from Society; and Stephen Crane soon set forth a corresponding hypothesis when in "The Blue Hotel" (1899) he noted that "Every sin is the result of a collaboration."

Thus the vortex of nineteenth-century American literary impulse throbbed about the divinity of man whose miniscule proportions in the universal scope did not reduce his glamor and dignity; about a principle of collusion which emphasized the awesome reality that suffering was a collective experience of the race and that mankind had "a permanent value worth preserving," no matter the price. The "malady experienced by a single man" became "a mass plague" to lure the "individual from his solitude" [6] into an inevitable union with Society. Like Whitman's "Noiseless, Patient Spider," Clarence Darrow began to launch "filament, filament" of "gossamer thread," hoping for his lifeline with humanity to catch somewhere in the miasma of "despoilers" and "despoiled" he had come to know so well.

[6] Albert Camus, *The Rebel* (New York, 1954), p. 28.

# Chapter 2

# MANIFESTOES

ON MAY 11, 1907, Brand Whitlock, American novelist and diplomat who was then Mayor of Toledo, wrote to Clarence Darrow:

> I am so glad you like my new book [*The Turn of the Balance*]; you know how long and how highly I have valued your opinion. I have never forgotten, and never can forget, how you encouraged me when I began to write; and that your confidence and sympathy stimulated me when I might otherwise have given up. And I gladly own that it was you who first opened my eyes to the truth about "crime" and "criminals"; that through you I came to know the cant and hypocrisy and iniquity of our system, and it was you who taught me not to worship the law as a fetish. All that is a debt I never can repay; and if anything I write or do accomplishes any good, or helps to bring about a better or juster order, you have had, and have, a great part in it which I hope some day to recognize.

The Honorable Brand Whitlock, whose major ambition was to achieve eminence as "an American Hardy" or "an American Turgenev," became, rather, a renowned Midwest political figure esteemed for his progressive methods of local administration and a world-famous statesman admired for his exploits as head of the Relief Commission in Belgium during World War I. The idea of being a full-time man of letters, however, never left him; eventually he published ten novels, several volumes of non-fiction, and contributed numerous stories and articles to the most popular periodicals of the day. Two of his novels—*The Thirteenth District* (1902), a tale of political deception and intrigue; and *J. Hardin & Son* (1923), a study dissecting the theological, political, and economic structure of the Midwest, neo-Puritan village—are minor classics of social Realism. At one time William Dean Howells himself asserted that Robert Herrick, and Whitlock were "the two most hopeful figures in American literature." This accolade alone would attest somewhat to the quality of this literary "amateur's" productions.

Clarence Darrow, beginning during the 'nineties to formulate and publicize his critical position, became Whitlock's acknowledged liaison between the sordid world of politics and the glamorous area of arts and letters. Young Whitlock noted in a letter to Miss Octavia Roberts, a Bellefontaine, Ohio, literary *confidante* of his, that the Chicago attorney "is deeply interested in letters, and should have devoted himself to literature. . . ." On another occasion the neophyte writer expressed his admiration for the aesthetic advanced by Darrow:

> I recently received from my good friend Mr. Clarence Darrow of Chicago a volume . . . [*A Persian Pearl and Other Essays*] written by him . . . one [chapter] of which was on "Realism in Literature and Art." His thesis is that realism has been ancillary in its growth to liberty, and it is one of the most remarkably convincing and scholarly philosophical discussions on the subject I have ever found.

To examine this philosophy of composition is to illuminate a singular perspective of Clarence Darrow and his relationship to the total scheme of American letters.

In 1899 Elbert Hubbard, operator of the quality Roycroft Press of East Aurora, New York, published *A Persian Pearl and Other Essays*, the only existing collection of Darrow's critical writings. With many aesthetic statements emanating almost daily during this so-called "critical period" in American literature from professional participants in the literary conflict between standardbearers of Realism and proponents of Romance, the essays by an attorney passed unnoticed. Yet Hubbard, then editing and publishing the *Philistine*, a weekly "little magazine" which delighted in needling literati, enjoyed bringing out the Darrow collection, for it added substance to the thesis of rugged individualism he had elaborated in the famous essay "A Message to Garcia": application and persistence enable one to surmount any obstacle. Hubbard set out to prove that a lawyer then surrounded by an aura of the tawdry and commercial is nonetheless capable of successfully

undertaking artistic ventures. Furthermore, this enterprising publisher felt that he saw in the criticism of Clarence Darrow a literary incarnation of a lifelong idol, Colonel Robert Green Ingersoll, American high priest of agnosticism who had recently died.
Indeed, Hubbard perceived correctly; Darrow's inevitable discovery
of this controversial free-thinker Ingersoll, whom he later described
as "a great soul of matchless courage, one of the great men of
the earth," defined the lawyer's responsibilities as a critic.

The focus of Ingersoll's little-known criticism was based on
the "Common Sense" aesthetic that had held significant appeal
for the American intellectual when during the early nineteenth
century this approach to the problems of art had been taught by
Eliphalet Nott at Union College and Timothy Dwight at Yale.
Two Scottish philosophers, Lord Kames and Hugh Blair, whose
huge tomes on aesthetics formed the cornerstone for this system,
had anchored their theories of Sublimity, Taste, Genius, and
Hyperbole on the Bible. Colonel "Bob" removed the theological
core from the Scotch aesthetic, and, with a picturesque vigor characteristic of his spellbinding oratorical wizardry, set down a
vividly exciting concept of the function of the artist and his craft:

> [Art] must rest on the experience of men—the history of
> heart and brain. It must sit by the fireside of the heart. It
> must have to do with this world, with the place in which we
> live, with the men and women we know, with their loves,
> their hopes, their fears and their joys. After all, we care little
> about gods and goddesses, or folks with wings. . . . The
> painter no longer crowds his canvas with the winged and im-
> possible—he paints life as he sees it, people as he knows
> them. . . .
>
> The great poets have been on the side of the oppressed—of
> the downtrodden. They have suffered with the imprisoned
> and the enslaved, and whenever and wherever man has suf-
> fered for the right, wherever the hero has been stricken down
> —whether on field or scaffold—some man of genius has
> walked by his side, and some poet has given form and expres-
> sion, not simply to his deeds, but to his aspirations. . . .
> The great poets have sympathized with the people. They have
> uttered in all ages the human cry. Unbought by gold, un-
> awed by power, they have lifted high the torch that illumi-
> nates the world.

The great poet is the instrumentality, not always of his time, but of the best of his time, and he must be in unison and accord with the ideals of his race. The sublimer he is, the simpler he is. The thoughts of the people must be clad in the garments of feeling—the words must be known, apt, familiar. The height must be in the thought, in the sympathy. . . . So that the greatest poet is the one who idealizes the common, who gives new meanings to old symbols, who transfigures the ordinary things of life. He must deal with the hopes and fears, and with the experiences of the people.[7]

The "great agnostic's" pronouncements on literary matters, while they revealed a tendency to evaluate art in terms of late nineteenth-century iconoclasm in their constant stressing of the follies inherent in "Creeds, theories, philosophies . . . prejudices . . . statutes . . . custom . . . Puritanism and . . . slavery of mind and body" nevertheless presented an attractive, fixed pivotal point on which Clarence Darrow began to erect his critical edifice. The crucial essays in the attorney's collection—"A Persian Pearl," "Whitman," "Robert Burns," and "Realism in Literature and Art" —recreate, as Elbert Hubbard realized, the imaginative enthusiasm of Ingersoll, but they also emphasize for *fin-de-siècle* audiences the immediacy and vibrance of Transcendentalism, then to most American intellectuals an obsolescent philosophical thread of a forgotten ante-bellum cult.

The "persian pearl" named by Darrow in his title was *The Rubaiyat of Omar Khayyam*, a work which, he tells, "remained unpolished for more than seven hundred years" until Edward Fitzgerald "carefully and patiently" made it "the thing of beauty that we know." The brilliance of this poem, however, resided most poignantly for Darrow in its thought:

> He [Omar] knew that man could not separate himself from all the rest of nature; and that the rules and conditions of his being were as fixed and absolute as the revolutions of the planets and the changing seasons of the year. Above man and his works he saw the heavy hand of destiny, ever guiding and controlling, ever moving its creature forward to the inevitable

[7] *The Works of Robert G. Ingersoll III* (New York, 1900). Texts of various addresses on Literature and Art. Especially valuable is "Liberty in Literature: A Testimonial to Walt Whitman," 251–304.

fate that all the centuries had placed in store for the helpless captive, marching shackled to the block.

Darrow felt that the poet was "not deceived by all the glitter and bustle of the world," and that

> He looked on the great surging mass of men, ever pulling and pushing, striving and trying, working and fighting, as if all eternity was theirs in which to build, and all unmindful of the silent bookkeeper, who could be deceived by no false entries, and ever remembered to demand his dues.

The flashes of truth purveyed by *The Rubaiyat* supersede all the philosophies symbolized by "creeds and dogmas" despite the blackest midnight it portends, for Clarence Darrow suddenly lashed out against the eternally existing oppression of the social schema which, in its basic corruption of man's integrity and value, possesses the dramatic conflicts necessary for the true materials of art:

> There was then [in Omar's day], as now, the master with all the false luxury that idleness could create in that land and time; there was also, as today, the hopeless slave, whose only purpose on the earth was to minister to the parasite and the knave; and both of these, master and man alike, were helpless prisoners in the schemes and devices, the machinery and inventions, the worthless appendages and appliances that bound and enslaved them, and that have held the world with ever increasing strength to the present day.

The essay, then, momentarily becomes polemical in nature as Clarence Darrow blends into his aesthetic the implicit responsibility of society in the creation of valuable art and stresses the need for a sanely balanced ethic that permits the Realism of the moment to clash with philosophical pessimism. Through the collision of these patterns of thought man generates within himself psychic motivation for his journey toward a spiritual euphoria:

> The pessimist looks at all the hurry and rush, the torments and strife, the ambitions and the disappointments that are the common lot, and can see no prizes so tempting as rest and peace. He makes the most of what he has, and looks contentedly forward to the long sleep that brings relief at last.

In Darrow's lead essay he managed to pillory contemporary theories of crime ("Every jail, every scaffold, every victim—is a monument to its [the world's] cruelty and blind unreasoning wrath"); he jibed at critics who felt *The Rubaiyat* too "sensual" ("Omar doubtless was very fond of wine and found in its use one of the chief purposes of life"); and he sketched his familiar picture of man trapped in the snare of hostile Nature ("All of us know how small and worthless are our lives when measured by the infinite bubbles poured out by the great creative power"). Within the fusion of ethic and aesthetic, heroics and derring-do as portrayed in the popular fiction of the day could not qualify as legitimate art, for the social being—the vital constant in Darrow's critical canon—was nothing more than a mass commodity packaged impersonally by the historical novelists and other sentimental storytellers for consumption by human shadows who sought to be entertained or diverted by the product. The spiritual quest for Perfection, however abstract, became in the hands of the semi-talents Darrow always opposed, a blind search for facile ephemera outside the day-to-day tedium of living.

As if in deliberate contrast to the aura of Pessimism he cast over "A Persian Pearl," Darrow, in applying his principles to a study of Whitman, discovered a "calm, optimistic, self-reliant philosophy . . . with its consoling power." The major impact of Whitman on Darrow, however, coincided directly with the "good gray poet's" effect on Ingersoll, who had earlier noted that *Leaves of Grass* represented "the true transcript of a soul" and "defended the sacredness of love . . . the purity of passion" against the attacks of "provincial prudes . . . [who] pretend that love is a duty rather than a passion—a kind of self-denial—not an overmastering joy." Darrow asserted that Whitman, in harmonizing "the sanctity of the body with the divinity of the soul," represented the "noblest prophet" rising from the ruins of a "sodden, commercial, money-getting age . . . of false modesty and perverted thought." The god-quality in man that sings "of the common" and feels "every beat of the great, universal heart" are Emersonian concepts that Darrow perceptively noted in "the material [Whitman] chose from which to weave his songs." The attorney thus came to utilize as critical yardstick the Organic Principle of Transcendentalist literary aesthetics as set forth most lucidly by Emerson in his essay on "The Poet":

> For it is not metres, but a metre-making argument that makes
> a poem—a thought so passionate and alive that like the spirit
> of a plant or an animal it has an architecture of its own, and
> adorns nature with a new thing.

The reckless elongated cadences of Whitman, "untaught," Darrow writes, "in any schools, unfettered by any of the myriad chords, which time is ever weaving," are "allied," the attorney continues, "to the wild chanting of the primitive bards, who looked about at the fresh new marvels of earth and sky and sea, and unhampered by form and rule and customs, sang of the miracles of the universe and the mysteries of life." Whitman's literary artistry will live, Clarence Darrow concludes, because of his "philosophy of life" which moulded, organically, his fresh, irreverent technique of verse.

Darrow then continued to apply his Emersonian hypothesis in the treatment of Robert Burns, a poet who, while "living in the midst of aristocracy and privilege and caste" was a democrat believing in "the equality of man." The poetry of Burns, Darrow found, draws one "nearer to the heart of the great Universal power," for the Scotch bard "went straight to the soul of Nature to learn from the great source, the harmony . . . and unity that pervades the whole." This dedication to the Organic Principle reveals the basically romantic side of Clarence Darrow's literary nature: Burns at once pictured the degradation and the dignity of mankind, its unfortunate docility and inborn aspirations. The attorney appreciated the power inherent in this human paradox and wove into his aesthetic the belief that man's hapless plight is best illuminated when portrayed against an alluring backdrop of extravaganza—the Darwinian dilemma of the race can be most dramatically portrayed when splashed against a panorama of Romance. The gentle humanitarianism which made Burns the master for John Greenleaf Whittier was to Clarence Darrow only a small part of the admirable poet's contribution to the literature of realism; the incendiary predilections of Robert Burns, his violent excoriation of Calvinism, and his enthusiasm in behalf of the

French Revolution were ethical traits that the Chicago attorney believed formed an integral segment of the poet's aesthetic. Struggle and battle, war and combat were the combinations Darrow came to feel most effectively presented the tragedy of man. He saw in Robert Burns, too, the dynamic belief in the god-like status of man; and relying on the Emersonian dictum once more, the lawyer was not interested in Burns' metres, but his metre-making arguments which suffused "the devoted poet's soul" and chanted the divinity of man's spirit.

Perhaps the most seminal essay in *A Persian Pearl*, however, shifts in focus from transcendental Idealism to the less esoteric sphere of "Realism in Literature and Art." The historical role of the artist has been, according to Darrow, one of a retainer "to serve the strong and maintain the status of the weak." Man's inviolable dignity, when examined in the light of Emersonian Idealism became a metaphysic; when examined now through the mundane scope of reality it was reduced to a working ethic aided and abetted by the doctrines of aesthetic realism. The implications of Realism were to Darrow, negative:

> It may be that the realistic tale is commonplace, but so is life, and the realistic tale is true. . . . In the ordinary life nearly all events are commonplace; but a few important days are thinly sprinkled in amongst all of those that intervene between the cradle and the grave.

Nevertheless, the truths derived from such negativism justified an artistic approach aiming to improve or alleviate man's lot. The contemporary objections to Realism Darrow found foolish:

> There is nothing more common than the protest against the wicked stories of the realistic school, filled with tales of passion and of sin; but he that denies passion denies all the life that exists upon the earth. . . . Those who condemn as sensual the tales of Tolstoi and Daudet still defend the love stories of which our literature is full. Those weak and silly tales . . . make women fit only to be the playthings of the world, and deny to them a single thought or right except to serve their master, man. These objectors do not contend that tales dealing with the feelings and affections shall not be told; they approve these tales; they simply insist that they shall be false instead of true. The old novel filled the mind of the school girl

with a thousand thoughts that had no place in her life—with ten thousand pictures she could never see. It taught that some time she would meet a prince in disguise to whom she would freely give her hand and her heart. So she went out upon this road to find this prince, and the more disguised he was, the more certain did she feel that he was the prince for whom she sought.

Here, then, is direct contrast to the dictum of F. Marion Crawford, leading spokesman for the advocates of Romance, that "Humanity, the novelist's master, bids him strike only at the heart." The realist "paints the passions and affections as they are" so that all people "can see their beauty and their terror, their true position, and the relation that they bear to all the rest of life"; he must make no overt attempt, in this age of "creeds and theories," to preach and lecture, for to distort fiction until characters become plodding theories is the antithesis of good art: "from the realities of life" are born "the highest idealities." No false manipulation is necessary. The realist, Darrow continues, "cannot worship at the shrine of power," for "with the vision of a seer" he perceives "the coming dawn when true equality shall reign upon the earth":

> The greatest artists of the world today are telling facts and painting scenes that cause humanity to stop, and think, and ask why one should be a master and another be a serf; why a portion of the world should toil and spin, should wear away its strength and life, that the rest should live in idleness and ease.

Unfortunately, Darrow concludes, "not all the world is beautiful, and not all of life is good." Therefore, "the true artist has no right to choose the lovely spots alone. . . .": "As he loves the true and noble he must show the false and bad. As he yearns for true equality, he must paint the master and the slave." Clarence Darrow solidified this position in an essay on "Literary Style" (1905): "the eager searcher after truth devotes all his powers to find this truth in the simplest, shortest way . . . [for he must] use no ornament or art that can in any manner befog or hide precious truth. . . ." Thus stood Darrow's bitter lifelong antipathy toward romance, cheap fiction, escapist literature, and other mass opiates to please desensitized enthusiasts of pulp writing.

The critical viewpoints set forth in the entire collection, then, fluctuated between polarities of Emersonian Idealism and Howellsian Realism, for Darrow utilized the inner force of Transcendentalist thought in approaching the spiritual phases of Nature emblemized by those numerous positive abstractions attributed to the Over-Soul; and he recognized, at the same time, a writer's responsibilities to faithfulness and truth in the real world of material collision. He agreed with his Chicago friend Hamlin Garland, himself a literary radical of the 'nineties, who noted in *Crumbling Idols* (1894) that the realist "aims to hasten the age of beauty and peace by delineating the ugliness and warfare of the present. . . ." Implicit are the social criteria for the evaluation of literature, the strong fusion of the ethic-aesthetic that excluded in his system art for art's sake as a valid literary approach. Emerson's "meter making argument" was the anchor that held firm the base of these critical sorties; but a Muckraker's focus on the unsmiling aspects of life distributed the lawyer's aesthetic between the organic Ideal and the dynamic Real.

When Clarence Darrow reviewed Theodore Dreiser's *An American Tragedy* for the New York *Evening Post* in 1926, he revealed that a thirty-year vacation from the tools of criticism had brought about no variation whatsoever in the fundamental Realism behind his literary pronouncements. The "somber, gruesome tale" of a youth's progress step by step from mission-house to electric chair and a girl's "from the factory to the embraces of the deep, cold waters of the lake" is "not relieved," so Darrow states, "by a single flash of color or light of joy"; the book leaves one with a feeling akin to "that of a series of terrible physical impacts that have relentlessly shocked every sensitive nerve in the body." Despite the fact that the reviewer was "held in a spell from the first page to the eight hundred and thirty-fifth" and that *An American Tragedy* "lingers and haunts and plays with [his] emotions as few books have ever done," Darrow realizes that the unfortunate incubus of sentimental Romance still hangs heavy over the fiction-reading public:

> Whether this book will sell I cannot guess. In this weary world people want to be amused. They like pleasant pictures, however fantastic or impossible they might be. They do not dare to look at life. Mr. Dreiser will not lie. He will not use

his marvelous powers to trick, deceive, and please. . . . The crowd will turn to Harold Bell Wright and the rest. They wish to be fed on lies.

Theodore Dreiser's "fanatical devotion to truth," Clarence Darrow asserted, will eventually gain for him the status his virtuosity deserves, a reputation as "one of the master artists of the world," even though he "may live and die poor and neglected" and "even though his art may be criticized and derided." The crush of Fate and the tread of the "inevitable" (a term Darrow used three times in the review) which characterize *An American Tragedy* evoked from Clarence Darrow an admiration which he had been quick to bestow on the literary idols he had also studied in the nineteenth century.

Three years later Darrow presented a final and most powerful summation of his critical standards before the combined presence of the Poetry Club and the Liberal Club of the University of Chicago. His lecture, *Facing Life Fearlessly: The Pessimistic Versus the Optimistic View of Life* reinforced his earlier critical dictum; now, however, the realism of Herbert Spencer, an evolutionary determinism prevalent in Darrow's fiction, usurped prominence in his critical views. The literary achievement of A. E. Housman, whose poetry Darrow had begun to study in 1910 when Brand Whitlock sent him a copy of *A Shropshire Lad*, became the concentration for incorporating into a critical aesthetic "the futility of life":

> The pessimist takes life for what life is: not all sorry, not all pain, not all beauty, not all good. Life is not black, life is not orange, red, or green, or all the colors of the rainbow. Life is no one shade or hue.

W. E. Henley and his "glorious boast," "I am the master of my fate/I am the captain of my soul" became targets for vigorous abuse:

> Instead of being the captain of his soul . . . man isn't even a deck-hand on a rudderless ship! He is just floating around and trying to hang on, and hanging on as long as he can. . . . [This] realization . . . almost invariably forces upon a human being his own insignificance and the insignificance of all the other human atoms that come and go.

The creative artist must be true to the demons of humanity and from this truth emerges Beauty, the Beauty, as Darrow puts it, of Pain:

> I do think that poetry is an exaltation and that you can't hold it for long. Poetry ought to have beauty and it ought to have music. You can be the poet of sadness; sadness lends itself to poetry as much as gladness. . . . The beauty, even if it is painful, is still beauty.

Housman's poetry contains for Darrow a meaningful union of "the painful and pleasurable . . . blended in beauty," a relationship clearly similar to Poe's theory of "pleasurable sadness." Darrow's brief statement on the technique of poetry, nevertheless, stemmed from little of the pseudo-scientific reflection that went into the criticism of Poe. Darrow always placed content over form; thought over structure; such was his allegiance to the Organic Principle. *Facing Life Fearlessly*, rather than unveiling a new Darrow critical orientation, intensified a picture of the lawyer as blown by nineteenth-century intellectual breezes, nurtured in Idealism and tugged by the capricious winds of determinism. Unlike his friend Hamlin Garland, whose literary radicalism of the 'nineties turned to a militant conservatism in the twentieth century, Darrow maintained his aesthetic with a dogged consistency. It was Garland who wrote in *Companions on the Trail* (1931) that "We [Darrow and Garland] began our careers on common ground, but he has gone on—or off—into a dark and tangled forest land." To the very end of his career, Darrow defended "immoralists" like Whitman and Burns; he lauded pessimists like Fitzgerald and Housman; he revered any foe of orthodoxy who endeavored to disturb the peace of the Elect.

In the early tales of Brand Whitlock is mirrored the practical application of Darrow's critical tenets through their influence on the art of a young man who looked to the attorney as master. It was Clarence Darrow who, shortly after making Whitlock's acquaintance, took from the aspiring fictionist the manuscript of a short story entitled "The Pardon of Thomas Whalen," offering to give it a critical reading and to bring Whitlock to the attention of William Dean Howells should the tale evince sufficient talent and promise. The enthusiastic Whitlock confided to a friend:

> Mr. Darrow is an intimate friend of Mr. William Dean
> Howells and he asked me to send him several of my MSS
> that he might send them to Mr. Howells, with a view to in-
> teresting him in them, and enlisting his powerful influence
> in their acceptance and production. . . .

Specifically, Whitlock had given Darrow a copy of a political tale
and put these questions to him: "Is it worth while, and if not, is
there any use in going on and trying to write one that is?" When
some time later the anxious Whitlock called at Darrow's office to
learn the verdict, he received the lawyer's blessing. "I was as
happy," recorded Whitlock later, "as though he had been an editor
and had accepted it for publication. I could not agree [however]
to its being sent on to weary Mr. Howells, but took it back with
me to Springfield, in hope, if not in confidence."

"The Pardon of Thomas Whalen," on whose basis Darrow encouraged the literary efforts of Brand Whitlock, actually combines
the method of literary realism as advocated by Darrow in all of his
criticism with a theme that would tend to have meaningful attraction for a criminal lawyer. Briefly, the tale deals with Governor
John Chatham, who pardons Thomas Whalen, a tubercular ward-
heeler serving time for murder. Whalen had been a district leader
of Chatham's party, and to pardon him will undoubtedly mean
political suicide for the governor; but Chatham has learned the
name of the true assassin, a woman. Despite the vulgar exhorta-
tions of William Handy, chairman of the state central committee,
that he reveal the name of the murderess to the authorities, Chatham for the present refuses. With the newspapers bewailing the
release of Whalen, "skilled and unscrupulous manipulator" of
votes, not enough unbiased individuals are available to regard the
incident with that objectivity needed for justice:

> "Oh," said Handy, "to hell with justice."
> "Well, then," asked the governor, "what do you say to a little
> mercy now and then?"

Most attractive to Darrow, perhaps, was the thematic concern with
the miscarriage of justice, for the breakdown of our judicial system was prime in his social thought. The writing itself in the
Thomas Whalen story was competent; the simple idiom advocated
by Darrow is dominant and the exploration of the shadier aspects

of politics intertwines unadorned truth without sacrificing literary motion and meaning. Chatham, a scrupulous governor, is not priggish, and his political advisor, Handy, is depressingly real in his selfish devotion to "party."

On another occasion Whitlock made clear his dependence on Darrow's opinion:

> The story [*The Thirteenth District*] I read you a part of when you were here last week is almost done. Since I discussed it with you I have lain awake nights thinking it over, and as a result have broadened its scope a good deal. . . . I believe that in two or three weeks I can finish it, and then it will have 50,000 or 60,000 words, enough to make a respectable volume. . . . do you think it would be out of the way to send the MS of "Malachi Nolan" to him [Howells] now, pending completion of the novel itself? Maybe it isn't good enough. You will know best—but I suggest it to you out of all my anxiety, and shall impatiently await your advice. Please don't be long in giving it to me, for I must be guided by your opinion.

Attempting to orient himself toward the realistic principles elaborated by Darrow both in private conversation and in his published critical essays, Whitlock in "Malachi Nolan" drew a sympathetic picture of the small-time ward politician, the "boss" who makes party wheels roll with a minimum of friction. Malachi's daughter Nora expresses a strong desire to return to Ireland, and the ageing political king-maker assents. When Malachi eventually leaves the country, the Municipal Reform League is credited with destroying his nefarious influence; but the abdicating Nolan knows better. He and Nora are on their way to the "old country":

> They looked out now upon the dull prairies that sprawled flat all about them, with no sign of spring as yet, but dead and desolate, broken only by a black and stunted tree here or there. At wide, wide intervals a lonely gas lamp twinkled bravely in a legal way as if to preserve the prescription of what was only technically a street. The prairies stretched away until they faded into gray gloom of the March evening, and they had left Chicago at last behind.

In the essay on Realism which so impressed Whitlock in 1899 Darrow had stated that a writer must "not swerve to please the world by painting only pleasant sights and telling only lovely tales"; Whitlock, then, running counter to the dictates of public taste, portrayed a scoundrel as his hero, set forth truth as he had seen it operate on innumerable occasions in political situations on the local level, and had presented it as a fact of life. The ward-heeler who manipulates elections is not necessarily a bandit of the cut-throat variety; he may be a moral brigand, but is he, there-fore, more dishonest than the reformer whose moral vision becomes blighted to the point of fanaticism? Whitlock took Darrow at his word: ". . . the realist holds that there can be no moral teaching like the truth. The world has grown tired of preachers and ser-mons; today it asks for facts. It has grown tired of fairies and angels, and asks for flesh and blood. It looks on life as it exists, both its beauty and horror, its joy and its sorrow. . . ." Malachi Nolan's adventures give fictional vitality to this thesis.

More significant, however, is Darrow's hand in Whitlock's first novel, *The Thirteenth District: A Story of a Candidate* (1902), a book which began as a short story and which was expanded con-siderably under the lawyer's advice. When Howells at last saw the manuscript of Whitlock's venture in this *genrè* he gave welcome encouragement to Darrow's protégé: "I am sure you have written a great, honest, powerful story. I read it with intense interest. It is easily the best political story I know." Some thirty-five years after this letter had unequivocally set forth Howells' attitude to-ward *The Thirteenth District*, Arthur Hobson Quinn, a contem-porary commentator, noted that the book remains "one of the best treatments of American politics in fiction." Whitlock's tale con-cerns the rise and fall of Jerome Garwood, a political opportunist who is defeated in the congressional primary after serving two terms in the House—a defeat inflicted upon him by an erstwhile political advisor whom Garwood had expediently double-crossed. Domestic difficulties arise between Garwood and his wife Emily, who detests the political personality a "candidate" must assume and who abhors the venality of her husband's knavish profession. Jerome Garwood's necessary "expenses" for campaign bribes de-plete his wife's independent fortune; nevertheless, in defeat he finds himself friendless and at a political dead-end, haunting con-ventions as a phantom from the past. With photographic realism Whitlock presented a vibrant composite of America's political

whirlpool: the rough-and-tumble nominating conventions of yes-
teryear, the torchlight parades, the stump harangues by gaslight.
His acute recording of truth was in direct line with Darrow's
stated major responsibility of the novelist: behind the glamor of
politics lies the same Darwinian hypothesis whose immutable laws
govern the evanescent and the perpetual as they do in life. So close
to Whitlock at this time was the shadow of Darrow that the
novelist could not keep the Chicago attorney from personally en-
tering the novel. Emily Garwood, in reflecting on her basic un-
happiness with life in the political bustle of a small midwestern
town,

> recalled having expressed something of this to a man from
> Chicago who had spent a day with her father. He was a law-
> yer, with a large practice, but one who nevertheless gave
> much of his fine talents to the poor, the forgotten, and the
> despised. For this he was called eccentric, sometimes crazy,
> often a socialist. . . . She remembered his strong face; a
> face wondrous in its sympathy, wondrous in its kindness,
> wondrous in its sadness. It seemed to reflect not only all the
> sorrow he had seen, but all the sorrow he had perceived in his
> deep, penetrating knowledge of life.

Darrow also influenced the veracity with which Brand Whitlock
explored the character of Garwood, who, infected by political virus,
can never really get it out of his system. Although he is a ruined
man, a new political campaign had begun

> and, in a spirit of what he called party loyalty—as one who,
> winning or losing, honorably lives up to all the rules of the
> game—he was stumping the district, and making speeches
> for the ticket with as much of his old fire as if he had been
> on the ticket himself. Long before election his old self-
> satisfaction had returned, he was as full of splendid schemes
> as a bumblebee, and if his disinterestedness was not so appar-
> ent after election, when he felt that his chances of being ap-
> pointed to a territorial judgeship were increasing . . . it
> may have been discovered in the fact that, as an alternative,
> he had revived his old project of going to Chicago to prac-
> tice law. . . . He thought that if they went to Chicago he
> might go to Congress from some of the Chicago districts—
> it was not hard to get into politics there.

When apprised of Garwood's idea for political reincarnation, "Emily only smiled." Darrow was doubtlessly pleased with the anti-romantic twist given a novel in which his aesthetic influence had figured so prominently. Literary propriety of the age would have, at the very least, brought the Honorable Jerome Garwood to the threshold of the White House.

In "Fowler Brunton, Attorney at Law" Whitlock penned a fictional eulogy to Clarence Darrow. Brunton, a "great criminal lawyer" and "a picturesque figure" whose "dramatic triumphs were associated with criminal cases," read "Shakespeare more than Blackstone, Burns more than Chitty, Dickens more than Story, Chapman's Homer more than Greenleaf, and the Bible more than any." Occasionally "he held high wassail and declaimed passages from Shakespeare, whom he knew by heart, or the long cadenced stanzas of Milton, or the all too perfectly balanced lines of Pope; sometimes, when the conditions were just right, he recited *Holy Willie's Prayer*." Whitlock stressed the simple powers of his protagonist whose eloquence and range captivated alike jury and audience; Lawyer Brunton "went on with utter confidence in his marvelous resources, with all the poets, all the prophets, all the romancers, all the dramatists, all the classicists he had ever read; at the will of his perfect memory, he quoted, recited, acted, and . . . dominated the whole scene." Fowler Brunton, "reckless, lavish, generous, imprudent, unconventional, a despiser of formulas . . . was a heretic and a rebel. . . ." He dedicated his life and career to defending those "poor weak mortals" especially prey "to mysterious impulses, vague, sinister, and terrible." His immense well of pity and his human love led Brunton to side with the persecuted; to defend the weak against power and privilege. Fowler Brunton, like his prototype, was a poet in his law practice who endeavored to bring the humanism of literary temperament into the courtroom.

Brand Whitlock's early contributions to American literature, then, reveal a sharply defined imprint of Clarence Darrow's critical aesthetic: the integrity of facts, the beauty of the real, the literary pleasurableness in sadness, and the artistic utility of sorrow. In 1908 Whitlock again expressed his sincere indebtedness to the attorney by writing to him that ". . . there is much of you . . . in all my books," and not long afterward William Dean

Howells, who had once identified Whitlock in a letter to Darrow as "that Toledo friend of yours," became convinced of the young writer's ability and introduced him with great fanfare to his widest public by reviewing the Ohioan's literary achievements in an article for the influential *North American Review*, "A Political Novelist and More." Darrow, by allowing his name and considerable reputation as a lawyer to stand behind the realist movement in American letters and by setting forth publicly and decisively his thoughts on art, had, in fact, taken his first step toward a prospective career in letters himself. Many a reader who otherwise might have regarded the clamor set up by Howells and his apostles as a mere transient aberration or another *fin-de-siecle* eccentricity paid close attention to Darrow's blasts against the contemporary taste for bad Romance. The lawyer's magical name drew serious consideration for any issue to which it was lent, so conspicuous was his presence on the American scene. While Darrow thus gave some prestige to the movement for Realism, he was still only on the approaches to a career in letters. It now remained for him to try his own hand at writing fiction.

# Chapter 3

# FICTIONAL JURISPRUDENCE

In 1900 Clarence Darrow persuaded John Peter Altgeld, the belabored ex-governor of Illinois whose brilliant political career was shattered by his pardoning of the Haymarket anarchists, to join his law firm as "senior member." Altgeld, derisively called John "Pardon" by his political enemies, was always idolized by Darrow, who had early been influenced by the governor's work *Our Penal Code and Its Victims* (1884). Darrow had been introduced to this treatise during his days of practice in Ashtabula, Ohio, and the Altgeld volume proved instrumental in orienting Darrow's steps toward Chicago with the slender hope of meeting an author whose philosophy of crime he had come to admire. Now in the twilight of his career as reformer and humanitarian, the "eagle forgotten," as Vachel Lindsay called Altgeld, became occupied with concerns other than politics and during his official association with Clarence Darrow's firm he began composing a work dealing with his "first Love": public speaking, an art he defined as "the child of democracy." In May, 1901, Altgeld presented "one of my children that the world is not frowning upon," his little book *Oratory: Its Requirements and Its Rewards*. Clarence Darrow, already happily under a multiplicity of literary and philosophical influences, now saw organized in a brief, yet comprehensive text book an intellectual focus he had at this point begun to consider seriously: the relationship of literature to the law. With the success of Whitlock's realistic stories as critical examples of this artistic affinity and with Altgeld's strong emphasis on the "eloquence" of "literary excellence" in so fleeting an exercise as oratory, Clarence Darrow had formidable precedent as he began to write fiction.

Governor Altgeld could no more write a book on the aesthetics of oratory and keep from it his political and social attitudes than could Colonel Ingersoll forbear seeing in Shakespeare traits of the late nineteenth-century American iconoclast. The concept of a beneficent "idealism" that contrasted with the "brutism" involved in the Darwinian hypothesis was adequately stressed by Darrow's illustrous law partner in his philosophy of the orator as romantic individualist:

> The world's great pathos is on the side of the masses who are doing the world's work and making civilization possible. They are the children of God. The orator must feel their sufferings, their sorrows and their joys. Here alone does soul respond to soul. The men who eat bread that is earned by the sweat of other men's brows are unresponsive and incapable of high sentiments or deep pathos. Wealth and fashion may be inviting and present a beautiful picture, but the divine fires do not burn there. All the great speeches ever delivered were protests against injustice and appeals for the public welfare. Generally they were on the losing side.

*Oratory* contains both the active, dynamic, practical side of John Altgeld's personality and the dreamy, inspiring, wispy portion of his nature as well. On the one hand he will italicize an abstract generalization—"Isolation is the price of greatness, and the stars are all the friends an orator needs"—and then, in down-to-earth, practical handbook-like fashion he will advise lawyers to "overcome" the "lowering tendency" that courtroom "wrangling" brings to their profession by studying "poetry, dialogue, history, painting, sculpture, nature, and whatever [tends] to ennoble the mind." Altgeld systematically emphasized the integrity of the written word and the major prominence of literary style as the components which immortalize the thoughts of an individual and which clothe his ideas in grandeur. "Literary excellence is the robe of immortality without which no speech can live," maintained the impassioned author; the ideas and the delivery may be of the highest order "but if it lacks literary finish" the entire effort will be completely forgotten "by the evening of the morrow." The results of devotion to the eminent minds of the past and to the principles of oratorical greatness, Altgeld summed up:

> It [oratory] points the martyr's path to the future; it guides the reaper's hand in the present, and it turns the face of ambition toward the delectable hills of achievement. One great speech made to an intelligent audience in favor of the rights

of man will compensate for a life of labor, will crown a career with glory and give a joy that is born of the divinities.

With his artistic vision pointing toward the heavens, Clarence Darrow decided that many of the requisites set forth in *Oratory* held true also for the literary artist with a mission. At this time, indeed, Darrow confided to his roommate Francis S. Wilson, "The one thing I want most of all to be is a writer." What better method for a realist to begin experimentation with imaginative prose than by examining the people and paraphernalia of his very own bailiwick? A sudden stroke of fate hastened Darrow's entrance into what William Gilmore Simms once called the "strife" of art: when William Randolph Hearst "invaded" Chicago in 1900 he hired Darrow "to incorporate the *Evening American*." The lawyer's profitable connection with journalism now afforded the chance to have published some short stories on which he had been working. Hearst did not pay Darrow for these contributions; their publication sufficed as the lawyer's reward. Thus was born *Easy Lessons in Law*, a group of tales revolving, for the most part, about two controversial legal points which Darrow felt were bleeding the proletarians of the day: the Doctrine of Fellow Servants and the Doctrine of Assumed Risk.

A legal guide of the late 'nineties, Fishback's *Manual of Elementary Law*, defined the concepts that Clarence Darrow dramatized in his early efforts at fiction:

> Risks assumed by servant.—The servant assumes all risks that he ought to know are incident to the discharge of his duties, all risks from negligence and wrongs of his fellow-servants, and he is bound to use care himself. To some extent the servant will be excused for incurring a danger under order of the master, but not if the danger be glaring, nor if it is fully known to the servant and voluntarily assumed. As a general rule, where the opportunities of the servant for discovering danger are equal to the master's, the master is not liable.

This doctrine is based upon the maxim "*volenti non fit injuria*," or, that to which "a person assents is not regarded in law as an injury"; thus, "dangers normally and necessarily incident to the occupation" of a given individual are undertaken at his own risk, not at the risk of the master, the employer. Regarding the Doctrine of Fellow Servants, the legal guide of 1896 states

> Fellow-Servants.—If the master has exercised due care in selecting and retaining servants, he has done his duty. If, nevertheless, injury results to one servant by the wrongful act or omission of another servant, the master is not liable.

With these concepts in mind, Darrow, perpetrating deliberately what Poe had called "the heresy of the didactic," began to educate the readers of the Chicago *Evening American* in contemporary jurisprudence. His *Easy Lessons* were fictional illustrations of the free and easy ethics he felt were dominating not only American justice but also American business. The title perhaps was derived from "Easy Lessons in Anarchy," the subject of Prince Kropotkin's lectures in America during the late 'nineties. (New York *Sun*, November 20, 1897).

The tales reveal Darrow's sharp eye for detailed realism of character and place and sensitive ear for the parlance of the railroad, machine shop, construction job, and coal mine in delineating the relationship of servant to master, servant to job, and master to job. This base of scientific truth he distilled with a crushing satire for the values symbolizing the Gilded Age, and with a warm sense of the pathetic. Following the dictum of Altgeld, Darrow clearly felt that the path to literary immortality must be best approached from the wrong side of the tracks, from the side of the downtrodden, the oppressed who Herbert Spencer felt were being despoiled for the general good of humanity in the savage advance toward Perfection. One of the basic themes unifying these early tales Darrow articulated best in an essay published more than twenty years after the *Easy Lessons* had appeared:

> I see no beneficent power in evolution. I see no beneficent power in the universe which says that of necessity man shall get better or higher, or what to me is more important, happier. I see with human life what I see with the ocean, an everlasting ebb and flow, the flow pretty clearly marked and the ebb pretty clearly marked; marked by an inexorable nature. . . . We all protest the cruelty of nature. And, yet, if we live, we must live the abject slave of this unfeeling monster which we call nature; she, to my mind, has fixed the limits of man and fixed them absolutely.

In these newspaper stories Darrow presented the universe in terms of a legal microcosm; justice became the embodiment of a hostile or indifferent Nature and comprised the system to which man must adjust and in which he must struggle. With the righteous ire of a muckraker, but at the same time with the cool detachment of a skilled satirist, Darrow allowed these little vignettes to be acted out and resolved in their destined conclusions by the complex forces of legal determinism.

On four successive Sundays in July, 1902, Darrow published four different tales illustrating for readers of the Chicago *Evening American* the pernicious and inequitable Doctrine of Assumed Risk: two sketches revealed the lawyer's concern with the major contemporary octopus, railroads; the others painted pathetic scenes of poverty and distress, the workingman's lot. Juxtaposed with the feeling and compassion expressed in behalf of the day laborer is the scathing portrait of lawyers, judges, and other luminaries comprising our system of jurisprudence. Lest one forget, however, Darrow in these tales was no mere tractarian but a conscious artist writing in the *genrè* which was to become prominent a few years later when the publication of Upton Sinclair's *The Jungle* (1906) made fashionable and acceptable for literary use themes derived from the shop rather than the parlor.

The story of John Swanson, Swedish immigrant, appeared on July 6, and revealed horrors of employment in a mill "owned by a man who did not believe in the tyranny of labor unions or [in] the right of state factory inspectors to interfere with his business." This master, furthermore, maintained that "he had the right to manage his own shop as he pleased, and he thought it a gross extravagance to waste money on guards for rip saws." This, despite the fact that the hands of his workers "came within an inch of the hungry teeth" whenever they pushed a board "against the whirling, angry saw." Swanson, with a wife and four children to support, could ill afford to complain about the hazardous, unguarded saw, for his fellow employees warned him that "if the 'hands' grumbled about their tools they were told to go." Thus, John Swanson in a matter of a few weeks made a happy adjustment to his new job. Employment, after all, was scarce and to be working on any terms was a luxury; the Swede soon was "as much at home [with the whirling saw] as an experienced lion tamer in a cage." He worked "as mechanically and unconsciously as a banker at his desk or a judge on the bench." Then, one catastrophic day as "fortunate" John Swanson

> was figuring how much it would cost to buy a grammar and an arithmetic and a geography for little John, who was just entering the grammar school, he forgot himself; the board caught as the saw passed through, his foot slipped, he threw out his right hand to save himself and laid his hand on top of the whirling steel disc; his hand fell off on the side where the waste pieces of timber were wont to drop, and the blood trickled down in the saw dust below.

Soon a lawyer "found Swanson" and "agreed to take his case for half the damages he could collect," but the Judge took the matter into his own hands, "gravely" explaining to the jury "Swanson's carelessness in assuming the risk." Darrow, sitting in the margin, commented: "The Judge thought that Swanson should have chosen to run a bank or sit on the bench instead of running a buzz saw without a guard." Then the mill owner, "a pious man," believing "It is more blessed to give than to receive," kindly took Johnny Jr. into the factory at his father's old job, and while he could only pay the child four dollars a week (one-half the wages Swanson Sr. had commanded), this worthy philanthropist felt that he was doing his small bit to help rehabilitate the unfortunate family. With an outraged sense of irony Darrow concluded his tale:

> Even now in his long vacation, when Swanson looks at his hungry, ragged family, and curses his ill luck, he imagines it was the buzz saw that he ran against.

If Darrow's *Evening American* readers were calibrated on the same wave-length as he, they sadly and angrily realized that Swanson had not run against the buzz saw but had been flung headlong into a judicial system corrupted by its lack of moral focus and humane equity. But this tale was weak medicine and gentle satire when compared with the story of James Clark, a structural iron worker whose fate was recounted by Clarence Darrow one week later in a story based on the contemporary truism "that a dollar deserves better protection than a man."

Clark, born and raised on a farm in central Illinois, displayed an early aptitude for mechanics and when he inevitably felt the magnetic draw of Chicago came to the city and found employment in a trade where ten years constituted the "average" life span of laborers: "Had he known this he might have chosen to be a banker or a lawyer instead." A married man with children at the time his story opens, James Clark, despite "a slight attack of indigestion" one morning, decided to go to work on a building which was to be sixteen stories high; he was assigned to a job on the twelfth floor from which "he looked down through the dizzy maze of iron to the ground. As he looked he could not help feeling what a long way this would be to fall":

> But it was only for a moment that Clark thought of falling, and then he hoped that the union would soon grow so strong as to compel the builders to put in floors as they went up, so that in case of accident the workmen would not have so far to fall. There had been a strike on this account two years ago, but the employers had brought new men from Pittsburgh and Buffalo and other cities. . . . Besides the newspapers kept telling the public that the men were brutes and were influenced by ignorant demagogues who made a living by stirring up trouble.

Some "humane owners" put in the floors, but this operation was more expensive. As Clark, holding his temporary scaffolding, catwalks across a girder six inches wide, he loses balance and topples over:

> It all happened in the twinkling of an eye, and then the people below looked up in horror and saw a man and a plank turning end over end, and falling faster and faster to the ground. There was nothing in the way except here and there a beam or girder, which they simply knocked against and then passed on.

After some weeks the widow consulted a lawyer and a suit was instituted. During the two-year delay between accident and court hearing the union supported the destitute family: "This was one of the criminal objects for which the union was organized." After the presentation of the case, the Judge simply instructed the jury to return "a verdict for the defendant," on the grounds of Assumed Risk. With humanity and the law as separate entities, the learned jurist never stopped to reconcile the fundamental contradictions that comprised his wayward ethics:

That evening the Judge went home and, taking from his library Lecky's History of European Morals, he read how in Pagan Rome the Emperor Trajan had passed an edict compelling a net to be strung underneath the acrobats who were performing in the circus. This was before Christianity and commercialism were born.

The next night the Judge went to a banquet of the Commercial Club. There he met some of the members of the beef trust, the railway combine and the associated banks. He spoke long and feelingly about the tyranny of labor organizations and his words were loudly cheered. He then drew a pathetic picture of a widow who lived near him. Her husband had been killed in the Philippines while fighting for the flag. He urged that Congress should at once pass more liberal laws to provide for the families of these heroes who die for their country. This was loudly applauded, for they were all patriotic men.

The dinner cost $10 a plate. Of course the Judge did not pay for his ticket. He was an invited guest.

The stark, bare, economical style of Darrow was appropriate for the pace of this tale; the unadorned prose quickly and effectively depicts the action as the characters are moved through their parts, and at the same time the portrait of the Judge, a true emblem of insensitive complacence, is taken with the deft skill of a meticulous photographer rather than hammered out with the crude machete-like strokes of an amateur assassin.

The railroad stories appearing in the same newspaper on the 20th and 27th of July again reveal Darrow's keen sympathy for the workingman and his union. By changing his name, Patrick Connor, a brakeman blacklisted after the Pullman Strike of 1894, eventually finds a position on a freight line. In addition to assuming the various risks attendant upon his walking "along the tops of the flying box cars and picking his way over heaps of ore on flat cars by the aid of a lantern" Connor must remember landmarks warning him of the approach to overhead bridges, structures built inordinately low so that the road might save money. Through a series of Hardyesque circumstances—an unusually dark and rainy night, the warning ropes blown uselessly out of reach by an ill-timed wind, and a strange black mist obscuring the hay barn which ordinarily told the brakeman to lie down—Connor is killed as the engine "plunged under the bridge":

The heavy oak beam struck him just above his nose and the upper third of his skull came off almost as clean as if cut by a surgeon's saw. He really felt no pain whatever.

The Judge, in truth, did reprimand the railroad "for keeping this sort of a death trap simply to save expense," but so long as Connor knew about the bridge, the unfortunate deceased assumed the risk and the jury necessarily decided for the defendant. So must it similarly decide against Tony Salvador, a one-legged immigrant who now pushes a gasoline stove on a cart along Clark Street and pops corn for the "liberal, reckless sort" slumming there:

> Sometimes on Derby Day or Chicago Day when there is a crowd in town Tony rents a faded blue suit of clothes with brass buttons and goes out on State Street and begs. It is strange how much easier it is to get money when your leg has been taken off by a cannon ball than when it has been crushed by a car wheel. This is because people are patriotic.

Through the device of the flashback, Darrow proceeded to show the events leading up to and through Tony's misfortune, at the same time painting in thick powerful strokes the picture of another helpless pawn trapped and, at length, shamelessly manipulated by American justice.

Tony Salvador, born at Belagio on Lake Como, grew up amid Mediterranean tranquility and beauty; yet, ambitious for more than his simple life—the "straw-covered hut, the little garden, the daily visits to the market square, and the few centimes that this small traffic brought"—he was lured by an agent of the transportation company into sailing for America where a job with a pick and shovel on the railroad gang awaited him. Eventually Tony drifted to Chicago and a steady job in the freight yards along the river. There, surrounded by a maze of tracks, towers, engines, and signals, he was responsible for cleaning the switches. The inevitable soon occurred. A complicated "puzzle switch" and a negligent towerman conspired to send "a mighty mass of iron" over Tony's leg. Literally chewed up and spit out by the monstrous combination of railroad and law, Darrow's pitiable popcorn man, now a penniless victim of the Doctrine of Assumed Risk, can be seen serving his customers from the "lodging houses, cheap hotels, second hand clothing stores, pawn shops, Chinese tea stores, saloons and dance houses, churches and missions, opium joints and shooting galleries." The little village in Italy near Lake Como is an infrequent vision of the far away and the long ago. Tony Salvador, Patrick Connor, and their companion proletarians John Swanson and James Clark were snapped up by what Darrow labeled "the forces that control the world" and were either destroyed or warped by them to fit the mould which antagonistic Nature had reserved. The Conservative Darwinians could proclaim that these sacrifices were all directed toward the basic common good, the spiral toward Perfection. Darrow's Reform Darwinism, however, saw little glamor implicit in destructive, though patriotic and beneficent, warfare for individual survival complete with rules and regulations. The carnage implicit in this social warfare being waged on Spencerian battlefields every day Darrow interpreted as manifesting the decadence of conservatism, though these economic skirmishes embody the glitter, trappings and fervor that "real" war must connote. The attorney seemed not at all convinced that this struggle for survival was the route leading to the ultimate perfectability of mankind.

With certain thematic and literary variation Clarence Darrow then undertook to lay bare the basic evils of the Doctrine of Fellow Servants and of other legal exigencies supported and condoned by courts of justice. Again the incendiary propensities of the literary muckraker were controlled by Darrow, who continued to write with calmer detachment than one is usually inclined to attribute to the reform journalists of the time; his approach involves dual motives, polarities usually defined as irreconcilable: art and propaganda; symbolic expression and mass communication.

His next contributions to the Sunday *American* laid bare further inequities of contemporary jurisprudence and defined in terms of legal expediency the influences that make the laws. On August 3, 1902, Darrow sketched out the history behind "The Doctrine of Fellow Servants"—the Case of Fowler versus Priestly in England, 1836; today, "Priestly is dead, Fowler is dead, the judge is dead . . . but the decision, bound in calf, is still busy with its deadly work." Henry "Hank" Clarey, a railroad yard switchman who later appears in Darrow's fiction as a character in *An Eye for An Eye*, is victimized as ruthlessly as was Tony Salvador by the monolithic railroad in a yard accident brought about by driving snow, freezing temperature, and a negligent switchman. As this switchman is an agent of the railroad, recovery of any indemnity from the "road" becomes an impossibility for Clarey; the company is not responsible for accidents stemming from the shortcomings of fellow servants. Darrow next utilized motifs of economic contrast and fate to recount another fable about the railroad and its servants. Millionaire Horace Bartlett, "a self-made man" who lived on the Lake Shore in a home filled "with pictures and vases and bric-a-brac" of the Gilded Age, and Robert Hunt, a railroad brakeman drawing a salary of forty-five dollars a month, are killed in an accident caused by the failure of a conductor to deliver a "slow-down" message to his engineer. The Widow Bartlett shortly thereafter received a $5,000 "out of court" settlement for damages. She goes to Nice, stops "using black-bordered stationery," and "is now beginning to take notice." The Widow Hunt, forced to battle in court for damages, eventually receives nothing. Her husband unfortunately was a fellow employee of the servant whose negligence brought about the wreck: "Mrs. Hunt is now doing washing for her neighbors."

Loading the dice of Nature, Darrow with mechanistic fidelity traces the origin of this tragic vignette:

> The order informed him [the conductor] that on the first section west of Whiting there had been some track repairing and cautioned all train operators to reduce speed to not more than ten miles an hour at this point. Just at the moment the conductor received the message he heard someone call his name, and, turning, he recognized an old acquaintance who had alighted from an east-bound train. The friends exchanged greetings and a few other commonplace remarks and then both passed on. There was really nothing whatever in the meeting, except that at the very moment when the thought of the message was on its way to the proper pigeon-hole in his brain this greeting seemed to switch it off and it passed completely from his mind.

Thus the structure of this tale holds no tension generated by suspense, but the pessimistic determinism places the principals in a fruitless game of Russian roulette and the thought, as Ingersoll would observe, derives from the sympathy Darrow endeavors to arouse in behalf of the brakeman and his family. In this "Easy

Lesson" Darrow effectively opposed the elegance of Pullman ac-
commodations with the unattractive and even repellant conditions
in the "coaches":

> Its crowded condition and the hot, stifling air, mixed with
> fumes of butter, cheese, chicken, and other luncheon which
> the passengers had taken from their baskets and eaten in their
> seats, had not served to make the car more bearable. . . .
> The sand and dust sifted into the day coach, where a bold
> passenger would raise the window for a breath of fresh, hot
> air. The ordinary cars were not furnished with screens, else
> one inducement to take the Pullmans would be removed.

The wealthy Bartlett, of course, rides in the sleeper with others of
his class, serenely unaware of the squalling chaos and peevish atmosphere of the coaches. Near Bartlett, for example,

> sat a pretty young woman of about twenty-two. She lived in
> Cleveland and was on her way to Chicago, where she was to
> visit friends. She was dressed in a tailor-made suit of a soft,
> unobtrusive brown, and a travelling hat which blended with
> her hair and eyes and the darker brown of her suit. In her
> hand she held a novel by Richard Harding Davis, while one
> of Winston Churchill's heroics was lying on the opposite seat
> with a box of chocolates.

Indeed, Darrow's choice of authors was not accidental. In complete
antithesis to the odoriferous box lunches is the sugary presence of
the box of chocolates; in diametric opposition to the bruising reality of the day coach are the flamboyant montages of Davis and
Churchill, romancers of the spectacular unreal. In this narcotic
literary haze, the young lady traveller—the "American girl" to
whose personal taste so many late nineteenth-century novels were
tailored—can effectively escape from the unpleasantries of the
moment, only one car to the rear. On another occasion Darrow expressed great contempt for the "women, young and old, who sit
and swing in hammocks, and read Richard Harding Davis and
Winston Churchill, and watch for the mail and wait for the
dinner-bell to ring." In any event, the wealthy Widow Bartlett,
without doubt, will be introduced to these authors before long,
writers clearly embodying for Darrow utter and complete literary

purposelessness and frivolity, men who avoided what Henry James called "the real thing," the real struggle, the real war.

Having explicated for his readers the "Doctrine of Fellow Servants," Clarence Darrow then contributed an essay of explanation for August 17, a brief examination of railroads as Forces in much the same manner as Frank Norris in *The Octopus* has Shelgrim explain to the bewildered and confused poet Presley this disagreeable, however basic, truth. Less symbolic, Darrow labels the road a "mighty monster." In terms popularized by Herbert Spencer, the Chicago attorney delineated "these new forces which rule and must continue to rule industrial life":

> A railroad is the personification of energy and force; back of its embankments of earth and stone are commanding brains and imperious will. . . . the marks of the mighty railroad run as clearly and distinctly through our statutes and court decisions as through our forests and our plains.

This arrogant monster, by "natural selection," chose the judges and legislators of our land: after all, "To lay a railroad track across a state requires special privileges." Darrow forewarned against the day when the railroad, through its immortal corporate life nurtured by the great aggregations of wealth and unlimited power would become the absolute ruler of our commercial life. The few who amass this wealth ("energy") under one control jeopardize the liberty of all, for such evilly-disposed menaces "are fast becoming the owners of the state, controlling not only its property, but its legislation, its institutions, and its ideals." Darrow later articulated his position more fully:

> It has always been the same story since the world began, and will be so long as the world lasts. Who will win? Will it be the rulers, fitted and equipped with guns, ships, policemen and with jails, always equipped for war? Or will it be the poor, the weak and the disinherited, who have nothing to fight with?

Clarence Darrow then revealed his stated purpose in writing fiction for the *Evening American:*

> These "Easy Lessons in Law" are not meant as a criticism to any class of men, but to give plain, concrete examples gen-

erally drawn from real cases of the way the principles of justice have been warped and twisted by our commercial life.

A secondary purpose was to brandish an angry finger at magistrates and their public image of unshakable integrity:

> For some mysterious reason [Darrow wails] the public has been led to believe that judges were not men; that they were not influenced by the same feelings, training and prejudices that control the ordinary citizen. They have freely admitted that the public acts of all other officials should be subject to criticism, but contended that the judge should be exempt.

Thus one monster spawns another, and the sinful collaboration between the "road" and the "bench" supplied Darrow with literary combustibles of broad emotional appeal.

The lawyer concluded his series of *Easy Lessons* by dealing on three successive Sundays with the unhappy consequences of the "Law's delay." The sad chronicle of John Rich and his family is ironically prefaced by a poignant quotation from the Constitution of the State of Illinois wherein an injured or wronged person is said to be able to obtain justice "promptly and without delay." Darrow, further, entitled the first tale of the triad, "A Story with a Pleasant Ending," for unlike his other despoiled, fictional clients, John Rich, a house painter, does eventually collect $9,500 from the streetcar company as damages for his loss of a leg; Rich does win his case, and insofar as this phenomenon is part and parcel of a just decision righteously rendered by our legal system, the tale of this unhappy accident is resolved with a pleasant ending. The painter, however, who had been fighting his case through various courts for many years, now receives only $3,025 after deductions for lawyer's fee and after settling debts accumulated while waiting for the streetcar company to pay off. With this sum he must take care of some remaining domestic financial obligations and look about for some new means of subsistence; he can no longer mount a scaffold to paint. The future for the Rich family (Darrow unfortunately wields "Rich" as a symbolic bludgeon similar to Hawthorne's use of "Faith" in "Young Goodman Brown") is grim, and in the concluding two episodes Darrow traced the subsequent careers of Jimmie and Lizzie, children of the sorry amputee.

As soon as the economic effects of Mr. Rich's accident were brought to bear on his family, the unit began to deteriorate with such rapidity and thoroughness that when settlement was finally and grudgingly made by the car company, the harassed father no longer knew the whereabouts of his children. Jimmie was forced to shine shoes and sell newspapers on the street corner where he soon "learned to swear and to fight" as means to survive the dynamic competition. Needless to recount, the early delinquencies mature Jimmie into a full-fledged "rough" well known to the neighborhood police. His career reaches its apex when he is sentenced, at the conclusion of the tale, to five years in the penitentiary for breaking into a freight car loaded with hams belonging to the "Meat Trust." Miss Lizzie Rich also finds her way to the lower depths, driven by the violent, coercive forces of socio-economic determinism. Quitting school to take up her share of the economic burden, she finds work at a cleaning plant, a "joint" paying $2.50 per week for a ten and one-half hour day. A few years of sweat-shop labor and Lizzie's

> hands were becoming crippled from the acids and alkalis used at the laundry, but while they ate up the poor girl's hands, they made the shirts and petticoats very white.

Darrow injected a soliloquy in which he repeated his stress on the all-important factors of environmentalism in shaping the mind and character of the individual:

> Almost everything in this world depends on opportunity. Take a young girl from the kitchen and give her a chance and she will develop into as vapid and useless a woman as ever graced a ballroom. Take a well-bred girl and send her to a laundry and she will have no occasion for her table manners and these will soon pass away. Heredity is the smallest fraction in the making of a man or an animal or a plant. Environment is the opportunity of the man; heredity is the opportunity of his ancestors.

Inevitably, the tale ends with Lizzie entertaining thoughts and dreams about the luxuries one comes to possess as a prostitute living in a "large home down on Clark Street near a church . . . [a home with] great drawing rooms, the fine piano, the pier glass mirrors . . . of such elegance as Lizzie had never even dreamed."

As the girl contemplates this possibility she observes her "one pathetic gas jet," her "colony of cockroaches," her "cheap oak bedstead;" in short, she regards her "lonely room," "barren life," and the "desolate winter" soon to come. Thus, the ironic results of a story "with a pleasant ending" and of "the law's delay."

The Darwinism inherent in the *Easy Lessons* is the single most cohesive philosophical component Clarence Darrow attempted to purvey:

> That man is the product of heredity and environment and that he acts as his machine responds to outside stimuli and nothing else, seem amply proven by the evolution and history of man. . . . This is not a universe where acts result from chance. Law is everywhere supreme. Every process of nature and life is a continuous sequence of cause and effect. . . . the laws of matter are now coming to be understood. Chance, accident, and whim have been banished from the physical world.

The law, too, has its own peculiar code for the survival of the fittest. It is with this hypothesis in mind that Clarence Darrow focused his literary attention on the grim Darwinism lurking behind the annals of jurisprudence. His tales attempted to instruct and arouse society to the peril everyone faced when caught, innocently or otherwise, in the nefarious webs of justice. A core of irony and paradox lies within these newspaper tales: the "easy" lessons, indeed, are far from easy. At a time when Lincoln Steffens, Ida Tarbell, and the muckrakers of S. S. McClure were also hard at work on various aspects of contemporary reformism, Clarence Darrow had incorporated into his socially oriented tales not only instructive themes but also a thoughtfully worked out syndrome of consciously artful symmetry, brutal in its treatment of the American dream.

Fluctuating between the despoiled and the grotesque, those crippled by economic determinism and those haunted by phantoms of the spirit, the tales issuing sporadically from the pen of Clarence Darrow maneuvered forth and back among the abortive dreams of slum-livers everywhere ("Cliff-dwellers," according to Henry Blake Fuller, Chicago novelist contemporary with the attorney). To the movement toward Realism in American letters Darrow brought those most intrinsic, fundamental demons that characterized a

personality formed by long and perceptive association with individuals in the "electric chain" of life. His tales ran the gamut of
emotion arising from the pathetic and sentimental misfortunes
implicit in his concern for the apparently inequitable distribution
of wealth and its social consequences. Darrow's sense of the tragic
grew in power, and two stories of the "despoiled," tales one might
collectively title *Easy Lessons in Life*, intensify the treatment of
those themes he had already embraced as the essential messages
his art would endeavor to communicate.

"The Breaker Boy," which Clarence Darrow wrote for the *Evening American* in December, 1902, is a homely story based on his
experiences among the coal miners in Scranton, Pennsylvania,
where, earlier, he had gone on an extensive tour of inspection
prior to helping arbitrate the labor dispute between the owners
and the United Mine Workers. With this story Darrow contributed his most talented piece of fiction to the Hearst newspaper,
for the pathetic narrative of Johnny McCaffery, who "was eleven
years old when he became a man," utilizes a structure of com-
parison and contrast, truism and paradox to portray with cutting
simplicity a picture of what Governor Altgeld had termed "the
cry of oppressed humanity." When Johnny's father was killed in a
mine accident, the youngster quit school and went to work as a
"breaker boy":

> Over the top of the slanting chutes was nailed a row of little
> planks like wide steps on a mighty ladder. Johnny was told
> to sit on one of these little planks and put a foot on each side
> of the chute and then, as the lumps of coal ran swiftly down
> between his legs, to snatch out the pieces of slate as fast as
> his hands and arms could move, and throw them into another
> pitching trough at his side. From the top of the great breaker,
> down almost to the bottom, sat this stairway of little boys,
> each grabbing at a chunk of slate as the coal rushed madly
> by until it passed the last boy and tumbled clean and free
> from slate into the iron pockets above the tracks.

In the dismal gloom of the breaker no one spoke; mechanically
everyone "picked, picked, picked while the black flood moved
down." So Johnny McCaffery spent the early years of his career
in the mines. During the following forty years, however, he comes
to work as a door boy, a driver, a helper, and a miner. Then,

emerging from the earth to spend his last years above the ground
—McCaffery's face is now scarred, one ear is missing, and asthma
contorts his thin frame—Johnny, now respectfully called Uncle
John, completes the helpless circle:

> Then he took his rheumatic leg in his hand, raised his foot
> until it rested on the right hand side of the long chute; then
> he raised his left foot to the other side, bent over and looked
> at the black, iron trough and waited for the coal to tumble
> down.

Once again a breaker boy, Uncle John was not endowed with the
black curiosity of "a poet or a dreamer," and he "did not seem to
think of the strange fate that sat him down on the narrow board
after the circle of his life was done." Indeed, John McCaffery
thought "no more about it than do the rest of us of the everlasting
turning of the great wheel to which all of us are strapped."

This study in pathetic irony bears adequate witness to the artistry of Darrow, for there are too many "coincidental" evidences
of conscious literary structure to be mere accidents. The tale is a
static one; the quiet motion meanders crookedly, but inevitably.
Nothing above the commonplace ever happens to Johnny; there is
no physical conflict or flashy type of tension to grip the reader;
the life of the breaker boy was, in short, dull. The artistry ema-
nates from the referents Darrow used to establish the dominant
mood of this sketch. John McCaffery worked all of his life on the
very edge of the railroad tracks where freights paused for a moment and then departed for the far-off places where dreams were
realized, glamorous cities that the little miner yearned to visit.
But John actually

> . . . had left the valley once in forty years. Then he had
> gone to Philadelphia, and his ticket had cost him $5.40. This
> was a quarter of a century ago, but he remembered the exact
> amount that he gave in exchange for the little pasteboard at
> the station window.

John's travelling is confined to a home, mine, bar pattern. There
was never a dramatic deviation in the humdrum routine that
characterized the daily burden of his gray existence. By repeating
the terrifying reality of the breaker boy's lot, Darrow grimly
blasted contemporary acceptance of a singular melodramatic as-

pect of the gospel of success then permeating with its deceptive values the scheme of American thought:

> Strange as it may seem, Johnny never had an unknown rich uncle who died and left him a fortune. Mr. Fox [the mine owner] never looked at his swiftly moving fingers and took a fancy to him and invited him to his home and married him to his daughter

Darrow thus used the figure of Mr. Fox (sly, cunning, hence successful) to effect the crucial contrast of the story. This gentleman occasionally observed the children working in the breaker; he was "lost in admiration of their dexterity and skill; their rapid movements and machine-like precision seemed to him the beauty and rhythm of a poem of perfect meter." Thrown into sharp relief with this picture is the same Mr. Fox observing the "daughter whom he dearly loved":

> He fancied that she had musical talent, and he found her the most skillful teacher that money could procure. Sometimes he stood by the piano and watched the girl take lessons in finger development, and he marveled at her dexterity and skill; but when he paused for a few moments beside the great long chutes and saw the black diamonds rushing down into his great iron pockets, and watched the little deft hands of the breaker boys, he could not help thinking that the piano was not the only place to develop finger movement. Still, that was about all he thought. . . . He loved his daughter and he intended to send her to Paris and Vienna to complete her studies when she was old enough, and, really, every lump of coal that rolled down the chutes proved how fondly he loved the girl.

Darrow does not sentimentalize the plight of John McCaffery; by presenting the factual recording of events as they occur and by revealing the promise which life extends to some, he de-glamorizes the concept of America's being to its underprivileged "the land of the heart's desire." The theme of travel, space, and brightness, epitomized by the young Miss Fox, who never actually appears in the tale, is set up as the natural antithesis of the restrictive, encompassed, darkness of John's hopes. On the literal level, Darrow has written a persuasive narrative with the force of a righteous muckraker. Didactic in its purpose, the tale, nevertheless, avoids preachment. The realism is colorless and drab; the underwritten imagery is sharp, blunt and economical. Darrow's use of pathos, his reliance on the natural consequences of so hazardous a life show how little he cared for the sensual depravity of a newspaper-reading audience—his details are lavished not on the lurid, but rather on the ordinary. At a time when the short story in America was being reduced by the happy hokum of O. Henry to the lowest level of pulp fiction for the appetite of the devotees of funny papers, Darrow, in creating reality with the care advocated by William Dean Howells, struck a blow in behalf of literary integrity with "The Breaker Boy."

In the *Pilgrim* for December, 1903, appeared "Little Louis Epstine" an illustrated story by Clarence S. Darrow which stands as the lawyer's contribution to the vast warehouse of Christmas literature. What makes the Darrow tale unique in this category is that the protagonist is a nine year old, one-armed Jewish newsboy from the Maxwell Street Ghetto of Chicago. Louis, one of six children, on a certain evening during the Yuletide season suddenly feels very tender toward his mother:

> He had never seemed to know how good she was before, and then suddenly in his boyish mind he commenced to think how hard she worked, what poor clothes she had, how she never went to a circus or killed a rat in the gutter or had any kind of fun. . . .

He decides to buy his mother a forty-eight cent string of "great red glass beads" he had seen hanging in a store window; "as Christmas time drew on" each day he passes the display to make certain the "jewels" had not been sold to "some rich lady." By December 18th he had hidden away thirty-five cents. The prize was now within reach. The Christmas spirit pervading the little boy, he leaves one morning for Newspaper Alley on the coldest day of winter. He is dressed inadequately in clothes given him by a charity—a coat so ragged that he always had to put "his left stub down through the arm very carefully, as a navigator would steer a ship through the shoals." Buying his quota of papers and assuming his post outside a department store, Louis realizes that the freezing weather has kept many customers from the streets; his one hand is soon frost-bitten and the floor-walker of the department store, "a self-made man," chases him out of the vestibule where the boy had sought temporary warmth. Louis sells a few papers, returns home and as he is about to forget the events of this wicked day, his hand becomes "prickly and numb." The boy is taken to a hospital where this other limb is amputated:

> She [Mrs. Epstine] told him that he would be well again before long. . . . Louis told her that he knew this, but it was so near Christmas and he couldn't get the rest of the money. She asked him what he meant, and then between his sobs he told her all about the beads.

The slice of life from the tenements of Maxwell Street is thus brought to a conclusion in the antiseptic atmosphere of the hospital ward, amid the germicidal odors so different from the "smells in the Ghetto."

As unorthodox a Christmas story as "Little Louis Epstine" is, it nevertheless contains, with a more equitable balance toward reality, the sentimentalism of "The Gift of the Magi"; but the Darrow narrative avoids the joyous irony implicit in the famous O. Henry tale. The social content of Darrow's story is obvious; less artistically conceived than "The Breaker Boy," Darrow's account of Louis Epstine plots the tensions of struggle and survival and reads as strong propaganda in behalf of the despoiled. While Johnny McCaffery dreamed of travel to faraway places, Louis dreamed of an overcoat: "Gee, I wish I had one o' dem." Both are maimed in the practice of their hazardous occupations, physically as well as spiritually: hard work and devotion to duty bring Johnny McCaffery back to the breaker; the virtuous honesty of Louis Epstine achieves similar results:

> He never took a nickel from a customer and then ran to a corner to get it changed and forget to come back, although he knew some boys who did. Louis' mother had told him that this was not honest and that he would never get rich if he got money that way, although the boys who did it always seemed to get along as well as the others, sometimes better.

Even at the age of nine Louis had listened to the misleading preachments of Gilded Age platitudes of "Strive and Succeed," for he had even heard of a man "who once sold papers and who always gave the change, and [who] was now a floorwalker in a department store." But the tale of Louis Epstine goes beyond pathetic irony and stands alone in the literature of Christmas in that its basis is the set of mechanistic principles bearing down on humanity in a most un-Christian manner. Louis's mother one December day bought him a "nice warm cap that pulled down over his ears, and [that] cost twenty-five cents at the department store." The gift of this cap aroused the feelings of love and pity in the rough slum boy, and he resolved to reciprocate in time for Christmas. Thus, the cap began the short chain of events that ended in the hospital ward; had Louis not intended to buy a present for his mother, he would not have been so fanatical in his devotion to the newspaper sales on so cold a day. Unlike "The Gift of the Magi," then, the exchange of gifts does not come off. And while the hero and heroine in the O. Henry story will doubtlessly survive their ephemeral problem, the permanency of Louis's experience with the Christmas spirit is evident, as Darrow was interested most in describing patterns of futility and striving that can be as brutally debilitating in the coal fields of Scranton as on the streetcorners of civilized Chicago. Hopelessly extravagant by the standards of today, Darrow's sentimental tale was made more tearful by the Oliver Twist-like illustrations ("No one stopped long enough to buy a paper," the caption read), but "Little Louis Epstine" was created as a deliberate antithesis to the conventional, stereotyped and formularized Christmas story established by the precedent of Dickens and perpetuated by the O. Henry twist on Yuletide among the four million. Darrow's was a Christmas carol for muckrakers.

Clarence Darrow found, as had Emile Zola, a philosophy of existence whose major tenets, dramatized daily by slums and law courts, could be movingly emblemized in fiction. Under the scheme of Darwinism, man held no significance, and lived always under the shadow of immutable natural forces. A woman by tying her shoe inadvertently distracts a trolley conductor who, as a result, runs down a passenger. Darrow brands her an anonymous "she," a "personal pronoun"; he states, "no one ever knew her name." Nevertheless, though Stephen Crane might term this *deus ex machina* an "adverb," Darrow's character "was just a woman." Both Crane and the lawyer, however, would admit her being a collaborative agent who, in acting out a futile role, has brought about the death of a fellow member of the species. All the radii in the Darrow hypothesis, then, emanate from socio-biological principles the late nineteenth century advertised, and the crucial idea of survival and warfare was the dynamo charging his entire worldly vision. Hank Clarey, a "fellow servant" who works in the railroad yards of Chicago feels that

> Tending a switch in a big yard is rather an exciting life, a little like being in a war—although not quite so safe or honorable.

Thus the theme of Darrow's *Easy Lessons*, lessons in "law" and "life," is, in reality, War: the war of the classes for economic supremacy; the war of the species for survival; and the war between writer and material, a struggle once symbolized by Herman Melville as a wrestling match with the Angel. Clarence Darrow quickly recognized in literature the potential of War in establishing a passionate tension to unify writer and critic in a single moral identity.

Darrow's literary warfare also constituted his thoughtful reaction against the Horatio Algerist philosophy of his day. From the 1870's the Alger books had been preaching to young and, unfortunately, old Americans the homely virtues that the Conservative Darwinians had been foisting on all who could read and hear. Typical expression of this ethical orientation was given by "Holy Horatio," as classmates at Harvard called him, in his introduction to *Bound to Rise, or, Up the Ladder:*

> Writing this preface abroad, after having visited . . . some of the leading countries of Europe, I am able to confirm what has so often been asserted, that nowhere else . . . are such opportunities afforded to those who wish to rise, as in America. We hear, indeed, occasional instances of prominent men who have risen from the ranks [abroad]; but what is rare and occasional in Europe is the rule with us.
> Let this thought stimulate the ambition of those boys, who . . . are hampered by poverty and limited advantages, and teach them that an honorable position in life may be attained by those who are willing to work for it.

With this inspirational purpose in mind Alger, with fantastic success, launched a veritable flood of nectareous verbiage on the sub-literary market. Though this frenzied scribbler died in 1899, by 1910 his books were selling at the rate of a million a year and the principles which he advocated were identified inseparably with the alluring American tradition of rags to riches. Even though Clarence Darrow had seen his close companion Governor Altgeld effect such a rise, the sardonic attorney felt that books "crammed with noble thoughts" were the most insidious weapons utilized by the opposition in the eternal warfare he systematically depicted.

During his school days in Kinsman, Ohio, Darrow had had his fill of the moralistic Alger-type protagonists who achieved their successes by assiduously practicing these admirable virtues ("Wait and Hope" is young Ben Bradford's motto) and, incidentally, by stumbling on some capital whether by rescuing the drowning industrialist's daughter or by saving the steel magnate from ruthless deceivers:

> We were taught by our books that we must on all accounts speak the truth [he noted in *Farmington*]; that we must learn our lessons; that we must love our parents and our teachers; must enjoy work; must be generous and kind; must despise riches; must avoid ambition; and then, if we did all these things, some fairy godmother would come along at just the darkest hour and give us everything our hearts desire. Not one story in the book told how any good could ever come from willfulness, or selfishness, or greed, or that any possible evil ever grew from thrift, or diligence, or generosity, or kindness.

In full view is the gilded fantasyland of Alger, an author whose preachments should have raised the moral and intellectual level of Darrow's despoiled youngsters.

The Chicago attorney, seemingly, set out in part to assail the neat moralisms of Alger as the downtrodden urchins of Clark Street come to grips with the same society that has treated the Alger children so well. Darrow severely restricted the arc of human activity, hopelessly unfettered in the subnovels of Horatio Alger: "Civilization is a constant building up of limitations around heredity; a persistent growth of environmental control. . . ." Such structures, Darrow continued, especially the "legal" ones, are built by the "strong men," and while any one of Horatio Alger's legendary heroes—Ragged Dick, Tattered Tom, or Phil the Fiddler—

might some day become one of the barons who wield the forces of life, such an eventuality was without realistic basis and with only a feeble case in biological mutations to substantiate its scientific validity and probability. So Robert Hunt, one of Darrow's fatalities in the "Lessons," had begun working as a brakeman with the shiny vision of an Alger hero:

> This position was to be only the beginning of his career; he was to be honest and faithful and obey all orders, and even do more than he was required, and it would not be long before he would be a superintendent and at no distant day the president of the road.

Now, fifteen years later, Hunt is still a brakeman "beginning to doubt whether he [will] ever be a president or even a superintendent"; drawing a salary of $45 a month, Hunt had been raised five dollars in twelve years. With Jimmie and Lizzie Rich the tale is predominantly similar: Jimmie, while selling papers and shining shoes, does not encounter wheat pit dealers and other speculators in high finance who generously lead him to his first fortune, but meets others like himself and must soon steal to live, for Darrow's people, indeed, are always unable to pay the mortgage. Lizzie Rich, in her meanderings through a sweat-shop childhood, never met the venerable philanthropist who flits in and out of the lives of Alger's children; her experience with social do-gooders is of a different nature:

> . . . sometimes a kind, lovely lady engaged in the business of charity kidnapped her and a carload of her companions and took them on into the country so that they might see what they missed in life. Lizzie always came back from these excursions thankful to get back to her companions and the streets.

In the real war for survival it does one little good to visit the enemy camp and become aware of one's own inadequacies for participation in the conflict. With the penetration of Alger's preachments into the catechism of American virtues, the rugged individualism implicit in his view of life deluded many a doomed youngster into believing that the American dream was within his aggressive grasp. Even Lizzie Rich was not altogether immune:

Sometimes a wild desire came upon her for some chance to live, a half-formed hope that in some mysterious way some-one would rescue her from the ever-present scorching vapor that hung around her life.

Alger individuals never had to wait long for this hope to be ful-filled, but Lizzie Rich, in one of Chicago's jungles, must go on dreaming nightmares of frustrated hope:

All night long she tossed miserably on her hard bed. Her sleep was broken and fitful and filled with horrors from which she could not run away. Now and then there floated through her brain the vision of a gorgeous palace with red plush easy chairs . . . then the horrible faces of the fat women she met further down Clark Street passed her in her dreams, and then she saw the river: then came a cloud of hot vapor and in the center a wan figure feeding a mangler—feeding it not with shirts and petticoats, but with pale, gaunt lifeless girls. Then she awoke with a start as the nickel alarmclock called her back to her basement for another day of work.

Alger's "classless society" wherein anyone with nerve, courage, pluck, and "sand" could rise to prominence comprised nothing but a panorama of crudely wrought directives emanating as if by con-tract from the camp of Conservative Darwinism. The breaker boys in Scranton and the newsboys of Maxwell Street were destined to wait in vain, so Darrow sadly declares, for the spirit of Algeris-mus to bear them "up the ladder" to "fame and fortune" in "strong and steady" progress.

Darrow's "Railroad," too, throughout the *Easy Lessons*, served to point up lines of symbolic warfare, both as a relentless force driving humanity to its knees, crushing the most helpless, and as microcosm itself, compartmented into several little worlds, each with a unique population. The *"emigrant cars"* filled with the stolid Europeans "chasing the ever illusive hope of fortune, which has brought the human race from the brute creation to its present stage"; the *coaches* carrying "common American citizens" who are still inspired "by that everlasting hope of fortune, and flee-ing from the hardships and hopeless obstacles they know to the illusive reward for which they dream and hope"; the *Pullman cars* which carry "the lucky, luxurious children of fortune [who] find every comfort ready to their hand. These are not journeying far away to seek for wealth in unknown lands. The fickle goddess smiled on them long since, and fortune is not a far off, doubtful dream." The railroad train and its symbolic connotation presented Clarence Darrow with a clearly etched depiction of his thesis, combining both a spiritually corrosive force that is of little consequence to the grasping materialist of the Gilded Age and an exploitative physical force that patterns itself easily after the Darwinist mold. In a random universe governed by the vicissitudes of natural law, the worldly counterpart to the machinery running the universe lay in the persistence of forces over which the railroad of the late nineteenth century towered.

The "structure and instincts" of men have not yet become adjusted to civilization, Darrow once stated. In the fragile values of Horatio Alger and in the frightful power of the Darwinist forces, Clarence Darrow saw a society in chaos lacking the most necessary stabilizer: equality before the law. Given an opportunity to present his case to a wide reading public, the attorney, fired with the zeal of a reformer but tempered with the science of creative detachment, wrote a series of fictional commentaries on law courts and lower depths, tales notable for their common-sense humanitarianism and faithful concern for realism and truth. He was ready now to widen his literary area of combat, for as his characters were in constant warfare with life, so their creator was warring with both life and art.

# Chapter 4

## MATTHEW 5:38, 39

*You have heard that it hath been said, An eye for an eye, and a tooth for a tooth. But I say unto you, That ye resist not evil: but whosoever shall smite thee on thy right cheek, turn to him the other also.*

During the first decade of the twentieth century the Theory of Non-Resistance had no stronger supporter in America than Clarence Darrow. By the 1920's it had no opponent more skeptical. To trace this philosophical shift in the attorney is to reveal Darrow's intellectual ties with Chicago Utopian writers as well as his literary exploration of themes involving crime and punishment, revenge and retribution. Indeed, at the Sunset Club, an organization structurally not unlike Benjamin Franklin's Junto or Poe's fictional Folio Club, where young Chicago firebrands and intellectuals read original papers, debated current issues, and planned literary and social apocalypses, Darrow's inclination to promote the Doctrine of Non-Resistance was powerful. Among these stimulating comrades, he came to a perception of heaven and the possibilities of achieving an "earthly paradise." Among the socially despoiled, however, surrounded by the maimed survivors of the warfare for existence, the attorney shifted this ethereal view and his vision focused on hell and its earthly manifestations.

In 1925 when Darrow repudiated the doctrine of Non-Resistance, he spoke out against that state of non-violence which had been advocated in the Sermon on the Mount and by numerous philosophers and divines down through the ages. While reputable intellects like Thoreau, Tolstoy, and Ghandi, with much publicity and universal admiration endeavored in the past to live by this principle, Darrow came to believe that the ultimate attainment of a state of non-resistance violated the basic nature of man and was, therefore, impossible: "[Man's] structure is fixed and is moved by stimuli like all other animals, and under sufficient inducement the primal emotions will sweep away all the inhibitions and restraints that culture has woven around him." When Darrow published *Resist Not Evil* in 1902, however, the lawyer had asserted in his brief preface that the major purpose behind the tract was "to state the reasons which appeal to me *in support of* the doctrine of non-resistance. . . ." At the turn of the century when he defended this viewpoint that he later abandoned, Darrow was moved by the current winds of Christian anarchy, whose prophet was Tolstoy, a frequent subject for the attorney's lectures at the Sunset Club. Also influencing Darrow at this time was a group of sentimental Midwestern visionaries then contributing much Utopian bulk for the Chicago publishing house of Charles H. Kerr, whose cooperative firm advertised pamphlets by Altgeld, Debs, Bellamy, Marx, Ernest Crosby, and some lesser "radical" luminaries: Father T. McGrady, an incendiary clergyman; and A. M. Simons, editor of the Chicago *Socialist*. Kerr, through his very active publishing house was to prove an especially able publicist for late nineteenth-century Perfectionism.

To persuade the masses—the range that William Graham Sumner once described as falling between Talent and Mediocrity—that Utopia was not a dream vision but a near reality, comprised the aim of ardent cultists who contributed to Kerr's various "Pocket" and pamphlet libraries. This enterprising publisher, who also edited the *International Socialist Review*, printed and circulated in a ten-cent booklet Darrow's address on "The Rights and Wrongs of Ireland" (1895) in which the attorney articulated strongly the views of optimistic reformism circulating throughout the Kerr "stable" of writers:

> The workingmen of the world are fast learning the doctrine of brotherhood of man; they are joining hands regardless of nation and of creed, for the common good; they are looking forward to that universal brotherhood which has been the dream of the poet and the nightmare of the king. In such a cataclysm, the opportunity of the disinherited may come.

The definition that Clarence Darrow gave of "Civilization" in 1895 foreshadowed the Christian Utopianism he came to espouse in the early years of the twentieth century:

More than all else it means the cultivation of a broad, charitable, humane spirit that makes a man feel a closer kinship to his fellow man. In the light of true civilization, all the wealth of a great city cannot weigh against the barbarism of hanging one lunatic in Chicago or burning one Negro in Texas.

Indeed, along with the hard-core, bomb-tossing believers in the integrity of the deed, Chicago produced from its hotbed of anarchism a segment of visionary propagandists for the imminent Utopia. Clarence Darrow for the moment became attracted by those advocating "the Garden of Eden, U. S. A." and wrote *Resist Not Evil*, a treatise published by Kerr in 1903.[8]

The concluding lines of the attorney's volume well bear witness to testimony that Clarence Darrow of 1902 was inclined toward sentiments of the Midwest Utopians:

Hatred, bitterness, violence and force can bring only bad results—they leave an evil stain on everyone they touch. No human soul can be rightly reached except through charity, humanity, and love.

Thus Darrow presented his view in terms similar to those employed by one Adin Ballou (1803–1890), a New England clergyman and spiritualist, who "stirred" and won "spiritual gratitude" from Tolstoy through his pioneer book *Christian Non-Resistance in all its Important Bearings, Illustrated and Defined* (1846):

All-perfect, independent, self-sustaining, unswervable love— *divine love*—is the principle from which Christian nonresistance proceeds.

The "bloody god of human injury" has been enshrined, Ballou asserted, "in the sword, the gibbet, and the dungeon." The aroused author outlined the major points Darrow would later stress in *Resist Not Evil:*

They worship him [injury] in armies, navies, militia organizations, battle-ships, forts, arsenals, penal statutes, judicial inflictions, pistols, daggers and bowie knives. And if we propose to lay all these evils aside, and go for nothing but uninjurious beneficent treatment of mankind, never transcending,

[8] Kerr also printed Darrow's essay "Realism in Literature and Art" as pamphlet Number Five in the Pocket Library of Socialism.

even with the most outrageous, the limits of firm but friendly personal restraint, lo, they cry out with alarm. . . . Great is the sword, the halter, the salutary power to *kill* or *injure* sinners *at discretion!* What *would become* of human society, if war, capital, and other injurious punishments should be abolished!

Yet the god-like injury sits at "his gory altar of revenge and cruelty . . . amid the clangor of deadly weapons and the groans of a bleeding world." Using Matthew as "proof text," Adin Ballou focused on a prime source of non-resistance sentiment; Darrow also knew these gospels well; not, however, as revealed documents, but as poignant delineations of Christian morality by which all men might happily and productively live, free from the violent pressures that the complexities of society invariably inflict.

In the first four chapters of *Resist Not Evil*, Clarence Darrow sketched his central thesis: he analyzed "The Nature of the State" (the "absolute character of official power" was begun "when the strongest savage seized the largest club" and is the same today "even in democratic countries" as with these early "chiefs who executed their mandates with [that] club"); "Armies and Navies" ("The teaching of patriotism and war permeates all society; it reaches to the youngest child and even shapes the character of the unborn babe. It fills the soul with false ambitions, with ignoble desires, and with sordid hopes. Every sentiment for the improvement of men, for human justice, for the uplifting of the poor, is at once stifled by the wild, hoarse shout for blood"); "The Purpose of Armies" ("the regular soldier is the man too poor and abandoned to find his place in any other of the walks of life. He is only fit to be an executioner of his fellow man"); and "Civil Government" (government "rests on violence and force" for "few can conceive a society without force, without jails, without scaffolds. . . . The thought never suggests itself . . . that nature, unaided by man's laws can evolve social order. . . .") Darrow presented a unified statement of social evolution, as he saw it, from brutism through militarism to bureaucracy; today, he lamented that the doctrine of Non-Resistance "is treated with derision and scorn" as a doctrine which, at best, "can only be held by dreamers and can have no place in daily life." Leaning towards Spencer rather than Freud, Darrow was naively able to classify and pigeonhole man and his motives into facile, easily perceptible categories; furthermore, using in his polemic "the unschooled child" and "the uncivilized race" as symbolizing those who perceive truth and "who obey the laws of nature and the laws of life" revealed Darrow's shortcomings as a philosopher and sociologist. Indeed, while Rousseau in the eighteenth century had had a salubrious effect on the devotees of innocence and romance—even on the American paradise-planters and pursuers of the Over-Soul who came later—the simplicities of Deism, Noble Savagery, and Fruitlands could offer no spiritual panaceas to the helpless, squirming phylum on the slides Darwin held up for the nineteenth century thinkers to inspect. It is no surprise, then, that Darrow at length forsook Non-Resistance; it is surprising, actually, that he ever flirted with the cult. And yet, the paradox involved in *Resist Not Evil* is that Darrow tried to reconcile Darwinism with Rousseauism; to mediate between naturalism and romance; to mollify Herbert Spencer and Adin Ballou. He painted the social struggle, nevertheless, in these characteristic terms:

> Natural laws rule the world. It is a mistake to believe that the conduct of man is outside of natural law. The laws of being that move all the sentient world rule him. His first impulse is to preserve his life, and his next to preserve the species. Nature planted these instincts so deeply in his being that no civilization can root them up. To destroy these instincts would be to destroy the human race. The first instinct of man is to preserve his life. To do this he must obtain the food, shelter, and raiment that enable him to live. His constant effort has been ever to get these at the smallest expenditure of time and strength. In a semi-cooperative state like ours the strongest choose the easiest, most remunerative occupations society can bestow. The less fortunate, the next best, and so on down the scale. At the lowest place, some are forced to abject toil, to practical slavery, to beggary, to crime.

Here is the Spencerian aspect of Non-Resistance that ultimately destroyed the validity of the theory for Darrow. Indeed, in his chapter on "Natural Law and Conduct" he reiterated his basic, evolutionary point of view:

> . . . man recognizes the great force in whose mighty power he is like the insect, or the grain of sand tossed by the angry

sea. Here and there he seems to dimly understand the great
laws of necessity, of sequence, of consequence, that govern
human life.

Spencer used the terms "evolution" and "dissolution" to describe
the building up and breaking down of social and physical patterns of existence; Darrow referred to the same evolutionary process as "sequence" and "consequence." In the philosophic dominion
of Rousseau and romance, such vocabulary is foreign. Yet side by
side with calamitous heralds of Social Darwinism, Clarence Darrow wrote these sentiments in his section on "The Right Treatment of Violence":

> Sentimental and humane thoughts and purposes are often,
> perhaps generally, based on real life, and have a natural rea-
> son for their being. To "turn the other cheek" or to "resist
> not evil" may seem at first glance to have no support in the
> facts of life, but after all that which makes for a higher hu-
> manity, a longer life, and a more vigorous community, is the
> true philosophy. . . . Man with his higher intellect and bet-
> ter developed moral being is much more susceptible to kind-
> ness and love.

Darrow made no effort to synthesize his material nor did he make a
conscious endeavor to explain the antitheses of his position in *Resist Not Evil*. The myriad influences on his thought and pen were
ceaselessly moving him, urging him to alter, to refine, even to
contradict, like the multitudinous Whitman. Simultaneously, Darrow was being led by the apparently convincing arguments of
Ballou, Tolstoy and Altgeld; of the Chicago incendiaries and
utopians; of Darwin and Spencer. To reconcile in his summation
such polarities would have been impossible for the most skillful
sophist; yet Darrow clearly felt no real inconsistency in this early
position of his: its essentials were presented not with exacting intellectual precision but by a heart which beat with "the universal
throb" he himself had attributed to Robert Burns. He stood behind
contemporary utopians and his first idol Altgeld in defining the
humanism necessary in the machinery of justice. In the moral
righteousness and spiritual efficacy of Non-Resistance he supported
Ballou and Tolstoy. In the necessary subservience of mankind to
natural law and hostile environment he subscribed to the theories

of Darwin and Spencer; and in his own final desire to see the system of justice refined to a state of equity where the integrity of man would be respected, and in his efforts toward perfection unimpeded by the artificialities of existence, the inspired Darrow followed many a dream-ridden poet climbing Olympus to commune with the gods.

In 1925 when *Resist Not Evil* was reissued, Darrow rejected the thesis of Non-Resistance in his foreword, but stated, nevertheless, that "I am convinced that this book in the main is true. . . ." Now, late in his career Darrow resumed a wholehearted Darwinist approach. The fervent, often saccharine, plaudits in behalf of love and charity were relegated to a position once described by the Reverend John Pierpont, another reformer, as he too wrote of an abandoned cause: "The lines are allowed to remain as vestiges of fires that once brightly burned but which have now gone out." Thus in 1928 Darrow with clear conscience debated the negative on "Do Human Beings Have Free Will?," the affirmative on "Are We Machines?" and the negative on "Can the Individual Control His Conduct?" He had come to feel that the utopian schemes of the nineteenth century were not calculated to be advanced by the realities of American life in the 1920's. The basic evolutionism of Darrow reasserted itself in the 'twenties, though, when he underwent, so Victor S. Yarros, a colleague of his tells, "a veritable intellectual revolution, caused by the study of Professor William Sumner's sociology." Thus, when William Graham Sumner "developed his theory of folkways, [Yarros maintains] Darrow magnified it and declared himself a realist, not a visionary, and realism meant to him acceptance of man as he is, with all his faults and defects, and pressing no reform that assumed non-existent human virtues, or mistook mere potentialities for actualities of behavior."

Darrow had been a "free trader" under the influence of Sumner, but by 1922 when the Chicago attorney published *Crime: Its Cause and Treatment* he expressed his belief that *Folkways* was an "important book" and proceeded to draw on Sumner's hypotheses and conclusions which, in turn, were inspired by the same fundamental evolutionism as Clarence Darrow's own basic outlook. The attorney adhered to the "Reform," while W. G. Sumner supported the "Conservative," wing of Social Darwinism. The noted sociologist, for example, strongly advocated, in the Spencerian economic scheme, which understandably endeared Herbert Spencer to Andrew Carnegie, the idea of unrestricted enterprise for Big Business. To achieve the purest evolution of the race, the strong would become stronger through the competition for economic existence and the weak, weaker, and finally extinct. Darrow could never subscribe to this ethic, and his Darwinism asserted itself in a denial of the validity and justice of legislation to encourage the success of despoilers in the ruthless struggle. In propounding this sorrowful view of mankind's bonds with traditional Darwinism, the lawyer adopted the theory of folkways almost as divine pronouncement. He wrote in *Crime: Its Causes and Treatment* on "Repealing Laws":

> Laws really come from the habits, customs and feelings of the people, as interpreted or understood by legislative bodies. When these habits and customs are old enough they become the folk-ways of the people. Legislatures and courts only write them down. When the folkways change the laws change, even though no legislature or judge has recorded their repeal.

This is almost verbatim Sumner, who apparently impressed Darrow with his blunt realism, his articulate presentation of societal selection of mores, and his division of the classes into a comprehensive diagram of mathematical certainty. Darrow was one to glean from social science that which he thought useful and valuable to his own position and to leave that with which he disagreed. In Sumner's definition of the "classes" and their "societal value," the "delinquent," along with the "defective" and "dependent," is relegated to the very bottom of the scale: "Every civilized society (Sumner wrote) has to carry below the lowest sections of the masses a dead weight of ignorance, poverty, crime, and disease." Sumner presented this thesis as an undeniable fact of life; Darrow accepted it as a harsh, unfortunate reality that society must soon bring under control. Some remedies the counselor now proposed in 1922 contained less sentiment and more workable humanitarianism than he had advocated some twenty years before. The major motif in suggesting ways and means of improving the penal code was, in essence, a return to practical Altgeldism. Sumner demolished

the Non-Resistance approach Darrow had for a time fancied. Now
Clarence Darrow harkened once more to the precepts of his be-
loved advisor. Society must abandon do-gooder methods of helping the criminal achieve a "moral reformation." Prison sentences
should be indeterminate; prisons must be placed in the hands of
physicians, criminologists, and biologists: "All indignities should
be taken away from prison life." His concluding words, more sensi-
ble and utilitarian than the panegyric of 1902, revealed with clarity
the sobering effect William Graham Sumner had upon him:

> It need not be expected that all maladjustments can ever be
> wiped out. Organization with its close relation of individual
> units implies conflict. Nevertheless, the effort should be to re-
> move all possible inducement for the violent clashing of indi-
> viduals and to minimize the severity of such conflicts as are
> inevitable.

Darrow, then, was able to use Sumner's conservatism to advantage
and thus realize more strongly than ever before that "social progress was [not] possible only through slow race improvement,"
through the ponderous inevitabilities of organic evolution. He adhered to the Reform Darwinist belief that "Legislating a better
environment, particularly a better economic environment, could
bring about a better world, and bring it about before unconsciona-
ble centuries."

*Crime, Its Causes and Treatment* was well received, not, however, without disappointment in some quarters. The Boston
*Transcript* while generally praising the book, noted:

> From Mr. Darrow one would not expect a conservative book
> on crime, yet we see little in his thesis that is startling and
> very little that is new. It is the swift strokes of reasoning on
> each of his subjects that make Mr. Darrow's book of especial
> value. Certainly we find nothing sentimental or maudlin
> about it.

The appraisal of the *Transcript* was sustained and embroidered by
Donald Richberg in the *New Republic:*

> He [Darrow] does not write over the heads of his readers or
> write down to them. He . . . talks with them, using the
> same adroit simplicity with which he persuades a jury into at
> least a tolerance of ideas somewhat strange and disturbing,

but appealing to the best of human nature. Thus he has written a dangerous and most entertaining book which will do no
one any harm and will make many a man a more useful,
charitable human being. A valuable Appendix to the Ten
Commandments.

In the analogy with the Ten Commandments one comes again upon
a key pivot around which Darrow fabricated his system. The psychological complexities of criminology were beginning to be recognized and clarified during the 1920's but he eschewed much of
the vast newness of criminology to maintain his viewpoint; he
adopted a humane, rational approach that the clear, simple demar-
cations of nineteenth-century thought and practice would encourage. Darrow still simplified the major dilemma: man's plight was
mere adjustment to environment. A voracious wildcat reader in the
"popular" sciences, Darrow possibly became impatient with the
new elaborate case studies and statistics that transformed into a
social science the common sense humanism that he had till now
upheld. Thus, even though he had given up the ideological neu-
trality of Non-Resistance, Darrow, rather than embracing a hypothesis embalmed in exact science, gravitated to a sound-minded
humanitarianism that was, essentially admirable in theory and
charitable in influence.

While neither Clarence Darrow nor his numerous commentators
have ever mentioned studying the infamous Chris Merry Murder
Case, it was late in 1897 that there occurred in Chicago this notorious criminal episode about which the attorney constructed his
novel, *An Eye for An Eye.* At the very moment when Kerr
Utopians were chanting man's brotherhood and setting up paradise
commonwealths blissfully isolated "among the North Carolina
mountains" where humanity in Rousseauistic splendor might derive from Nature a spiritual basis for Perfection, the frightening
image of Chris Merry burst before a horrified, then vengeful, public. Merry, a leader in the Henry Street Gang that flourished in the
"Bloody Maxwell" area of the Chicago underworld, kicked "his in-
valid wife to death." For this crime he was indicted, tried, and
hanged. The violent incident, apparently, contained some magnetic, seminal possibilities for Darrow, and it seems that the lawyer discovered numerous socio-literary attractions implicit in the
trial. He closely followed the final stages in the dubious career of

this "celebrated" Chris Merry, who was described by the State criminologist as the "choicest flower ever garnered from this field of crime" and by a local newspaper as "one of the worst criminals that ever lived in Chicago"—no mean distinction, even in 1898.

Merry was raised in a "terror district swarming with hoodlums, cop fighters, footpads, [and] burglars." As a youth he was a "ferocious rough and tumble fighter" under whose aggressive leadership the Henry Street Gang "became the most successful thieving outfit in the city." His apparent occupation was peddler, "but the wagon he drove . . . was little more than a receptacle for stolen goods and a means of flight." Chris Merry also "was subject to terrible fits of anger on little or no provocation," during which times, the Chicago *Tribune* once reported, "he became a demon unleashed, and acted more like a mad animal than like a human being." This atavism, part and parcel of his "habitually sullen and morose" personality, frequently led Merry to sudden fits of erratic, reckless, uncontrollable behavior where he became a passive entity entirely at the mercy of his unpredictable impulses. At such moments, Darrow perceived, Merry was a helpless victim of biological phenomena coursing through his very being, closely resembling a devout in the throes of a mystical religious experience.

The Chicago *Daily Tribune* for January 22, 1898, with a series of headlines, outlined the plight of this wife-killer:

## MERRY IS TO HANG
### JURY FINDS HIM GUILTY OF THE
### MURDER OF HIS WIFE

### SHORT WORK ON UXORICIDE

### CONDEMNED MAN'S MOTHER SEES HIM
### IN HIS CELL

### HE SNEERS OPENLY AT THE LAW

The story that followed revealed a collision of man and force, the type of which was to become the sustaining problem of *An Eye for An Eye:*

> Death for Chris Merry . . . was the verdict which the jury reported to Judge Horton at ten o'clock yesterday morning. . . . One ballot only was necessary to settle Merry's guilt

and one more to fix the penalty at death. . . . Merry quaked, his face was pallid, and he looked at no one. When the clerk read the verdict finding Chris Merry guilty of the murder of his wife, Pauline Merry, as charged . . . perspiration started from every pore in Merry's face. . . .

Merry was practically deserted, save for his guard, who remained by his side. . . . Merry was taken from cell 309, which he occupied since his incarceration, to cell 226 on the second tier. This is one of three cells specially constructed for condemned prisoners. There are bars at each end of the cell, and a perfect view of the interior is to be had at all times. J. F. O'Neal was detailed as death watch during the afternoon.

### MERRY'S MOTHER SEES HER SON

Merry's mother called upon him at 1 o'clock. She shed tears as she moaned: "O, my son! My son! To think you would come to this." Merry was considerably affected by the interview in the death chamber. "O, there's no use of my talking about this matter," said Merry later. "I didn't have a fair trial. Law——," he sneered. "They hustled me along to the gallows from the day I was arrested. I wasn't given any sort of a chance. I didn't testify because I saw it was useless. My testimony would have done no good. When the final scene comes I'll show them who has nerve."

The bereaved parent, the allegedly victimized murderer, the swiftly uncompromising, inhumane process of law merged into a befuddled pattern of charged emotion. An "underdog" caught in the web of social complicity became clear to Clarence Darrow. The news story of the sentencing added a highly dramatic flourish in recounting an almost theatrical series of coincidences attendant upon the case:

### MURDERER BETRAYS NO EMOTION WHEN JUDGE HORTON SENTENCES HIM— FRIDAY FIGURES PROMINENTLY IN CASE

Chris Merry was sentenced yesterday by Judge Horton to be hanged on Friday, February 18, for the murder of his wife. The execution will take place just three months less one day after the crime was committed. Merry showed no feeling when his sentence was pronounced. The courtroom was

crowded, and many expected the prisoner to break down, but
he did not falter.

In pronouncing sentence Judge Horton said it was the most
brutal murder ever tried before him. There were, he said, no
extenuating circumstances. Friday has figured prominently in
the Merry Case. On Friday, November 12, he was arrested
and fined $50 for beating his wife. On Friday, November 19,
he enticed the woman to their home, 50 Hope Street, and
killed her. On Friday, December 19, he was arrested and
identified in Princeton, Kentucky. On Friday, January 21, a
jury found him guilty, and yesterday he was sentenced to
hang on Friday, February 18.

Elements of flight and pursuit were thus added to this criminal pattern now studied by Darrow; the inevitable tread of fateful Friday,
too, held fascinating appeal for a lawyer so attuned to the curious
footsteps of destiny that doggedly pursue those unfortunates who
have even for a moment stepped aside from the brotherhood of
man and left a void which they can no longer occupy.

The New York *Tribune* reported the sentencing of "Chris
Merry, the pedler [sic] recently convicted of beating and choking
his wife . . . to death" and noted that the date set for his execution "is barely outside the limit of time allowed by statute to con-
demn murderers." The *Tribune* also noted that "Merry's attorneys
made the usual motions for a new trial and arrest of the sentence,
which were overruled, the Court stating there was absolutely no
grounds for them." On February 17, however, Governor Tanner
postponed the hanging for sixty days "in order to have the Supreme Court or Board of Pardons look into the matter." The Chicago *Daily News* described Merry the day before his expected execution and the moment he learned of the postponement:

> When the Chicago authorities received . . . the intelligence
> of the governor's action Merry was lying upon a small cot in
> the death chamber, to which he had been removed this morn-
> ing. . . . Something in the face of the visitor told Merry
> what was coming for his eyes brightened and the despondency
> veiling his features disappeared, while a deep flush appeared
> on his cheeks. . . .
> [On Merry's hearing the news], the blood surged faster into
> his face, but with customary self-control he made no comment
> and allowed no unwonted agitation to convulse his features.

Slowly loosening his arms, which had been clasped under his head, he arose and, sitting upon the edge of the cot, with his hands stretched straight at his sides and his head sunk deep between his shoulders, he gazed slowly about him. His glance traveled across the floor and rested for a moment on the tall, stony-featured death watch sitting with eyes bent upon him, and then wandered to the window, against which rain was beginning to patter. . . .

He beamed genially upon his informants, relapsed into a half reverie, in which he smiled to himself a couple of times, and then the gravity of the impending crisis of tomorrow morning, from which he had been rescued for a while, seemingly burst upon him with great force and his face became transfigured with emotion. . . .

He was informed that for the day he would remain in the death chamber and after nodding reflectively a couple of times he lay down again and, reclining at length with his eyes staring straight at the ceiling above him, relapsed into a silent mood.

While Clarence Darrow's convicted murderer received no stay of execution, his days awaiting death were characterized by behavior qualms similar to Merry's understandable manic depressiveness. The lawyer, furthermore, with an eye cocked toward the literary possibilities of the Merry Case, paid close attention to the final paragraph in the story printed by the *News:*

Work on the gallows on which Chris Merry was to perish had been begun. Jailer Whitman superintended the work and it was carried on with swiftness. That portion constructed before the news of the stay was received will not be torn down, but will be allowed to stand in anticipation of need at the expiration of the respite.

The "redoubtable" Chris Merry, who had become a legend of underworld folklore for once fighting "a two-hour pistol battle with a posse of policemen" was eventually executed for a crime which outraged even the chronically sentimental well-wishers of all notorious outlaws. Merry's unhappy fate, then, left Clarence Darrow with a residue of literary potential evolved from the strange, factual episode. The motivation for the crime, its crude completion; the succession of Friday misfortunes, the flight and pursuit; the vigil for a pardon, the preparations for execution—all the most spectacular anomalies of the case, Darrow felt, could be laced together into a fictional narrative made cohesive by Fate and Social Complicity. He had found a vehicle for the purveyance of his criminological theories as well as his literary orientation. Mrs. Darrow tells something about the inspired composition of *An Eye for An Eye:*

> He wrote it sitting on logs in the Colorado mountains, while we'd rest from long tramps. He'd write at the foot of some beguiling mountain, scribbling away while he drank in the beauty of the vista. He finished it in two weeks or a little more.

Published in 1905 by the Fox, Duffield Company of New York, Darrow's novel was almost simultaneously issued in a fifty-cent edition by the Wilshire Book Company, a Gotham firm which advertised itself as the "Clearing House for all Socialist Literature." Asserted the publisher: "Darrow as an Orator and an Advocate We Know—Darrow, the Author, We All Want to Know."

*An Eye for An Eye* relates with a stringent, compressive singularity of theme and purpose a tale of murder and retribution, which, without moralizing, delineates the pathos and terror essential to Social Darwinism and the brutalizing struggle for existence of any lower case man trapped in an upper case Universe. The novel, furthermore, illuminates Darrow's literary concern with what Frank Norris, a contemporary American author of the era, explained as "the responsibilities of the novelist":

> The people have a right to the truth as they have a right to life, liberty, and the pursuit of happiness. It is *not* right that they be exploited and deceived with false morality, false history, false philosophy, false emotions, false heroism, false notions of self-sacrifice, false views of religion, of duty, of conduct, and of manners.

Darrow in this novel oriented himself toward the truth of the Muckraker. Said one critic, "It [the novel] gives one a painful insight into the debasing influences of a life of poverty and suffering, and shows how society and not her victims should be answerable for such unpremeditated crimes." The book achieved, according to another commentator, "a more severe arraignment of social conditions than the fiercest tirades could be." At the same time *An Eye for An Eye* marked for the attorney a serious venture into sustained fiction, an area where the crudities and shortcomings of a novice are not so easily obscured as they might be in newspaper short stories. He emerged from his bout with Art, however, deserving a trophy not only for sociological veracity but also for genuine literary achievement.

*An Eye for An Eye* takes place in Chicago and maintains with this geographical center the classic Aristotelian unities of Time, Place, and Action. Jim Jackson, the protagonist, is permitted to present in his own defense textures of background, circumstance, and condition that he had failed to lay bare in the witness box. Jackson, in a cell on death row, by recounting the details leading up to and following the murder of his wife, comes to achieve on the night before his appointment with the hangman an emotional purgation, the type of catharsis he could not reach with a priest. As he talks to his visiting friend Hank Clery (the spelling of his name altered somewhat from the *Easy Lessons*) in the grim, sweaty solitude of his prison cell, Jackson hears the gallows being constructed, listens for the dropping of test sandbags to assure the strength of the rope, and hopefully awaits a last minute reprieve from the office of the governor. Two points of view, then, are established early in the novel: Jackson's precise statement of the causative factors leading up to his crime; and Hank Clery's ultimate understanding of and sympathy for a human dilemma that has made his visit to the prison not "an errand of mercy," but a moment of truth, enlightenment and emotional growth:

> I didn't know how it was—[Clery says] when I come I felt as if you'd been awful bad, and of course I know it wa'n't right, but somehow I know it might have happened to me, or 'most anybody, almost, and that you ain't so bad. I can't tell you anything about how I feel, but I'm glad I come. It's done me good.

Through these illiterate, nevertheless articulate, spokesmen, Clarence Darrow's art and thought are unfolded.

Jim Jackson was an orphan raised by a poor aunt and educated through the sixth grade; as a boy his neighborhood idols were the aldermen and other political workers who were entitled to be called "Honorable." At fourteen Jackson was working in the stock-yards, but unable to stomach the butchery there, he quit for a job as switchman for the railroad. Soon he was at home in the yards, weathered various strikes, survived a blacklisting, and at length married the waitress in a neighborhood eatery, a girl Jim had not particularly noticed until, he recounts, "the time she got that red waist and done her hair up with them red ribbons. I don't know anything about how it was, but them seemed to ketch my eye and I commenced goin' with her. . . ." Conditions immediately con-spired to thwart the rosy plans of the newlyweds. Economic pov-erty is always a major demon; Jackson quits the railroad, and, buy-ing a horse and cart, he becomes a street peddler of potatoes and other vegetables, generally of a sub-standard nature, unfit for sale in regular markets. Life is complicated even more by the birth of a son. Quarrels between Jim and his wife now grow in fre-quency and intensity. Before the birth of their child both had, in a lucid moment, calmly admitted to an impulsive mistake and de-cided on a divorce; but the beleaguered family was stymied again by a collaboration of pressures: the settlement house to which they appealed for advice opposed the divorce; the Roman Catholic priest of whom they sought religious counsel warned against it; and the willing lawyer who agreed to handle the proceedings asked for fifty dollars, to the Jacksons a prohibitively astronomical fig-ure. They decided to stay together, but their sorry lot did not im-prove.

Jim comes home one evening, having been treated to several rounds of drinks by some local politicians seeking reelection. The tired peddler had brought home a piece of steak for the family sup-per. His wife, disturbed at the reek of liquor and at the extrava-gance of steak, admonishes him. He, in turn, later reprimands her for ruining, rather than "cooking" the meat. After the boy is put to bed, the quarrel continues, with both becoming hysterical be-yond reason until after Mrs. Jackson brands him a coward and dares Jim to kill her, he blindly seizes a coal poker and strikes her on the forehead. Jackson, then, having crossed into the zone of crime finds himself in a world where he does not know how to function. He can only think of flight and of disposing of the body, which he wraps in a blanket and loads onto his peddling cart. The frenzied killer drives to the outskirts of the city where he drops the corpse into what he believes is a deep, secluded gulley far from

the haunts of everyone. Then, in another amateurish move, Jim
drives his cart back home, leaves his sleeping child, and hops a
freight south. Four days later after riding inside a single box-car
shunted from one line to another, the fugitive arrives in Mississippi. Here he finds employment in a lumber mill, but in a few
days news of the horrible Chicago murder filters through to the
South and the fidgity Jackson begins skipping from one job to
another—leaving as soon as any one curiously inquires about his
home town or his past. A reward of one thousand dollars has by
now been placed on his head, as Chicago bellows vengeance.

Finally Jim is picked up as a vagrant, taken to jail in a Mississippi hamlet and at length identified by the local officers of the law.
Soon he is returned to Chicago to stand trial, a city, as Fate would
have it, then caught in the excitement of a purity crusade run by
the Anti-Crimes Committee. The city was further whipped into
a foaming frenzy by the newspapers which had been portraying
Jackson as a psychopathic, homicidal maniac who terrorized all
the law enforcement agencies of the South before dare-devil police, after a "desperate fight," overpowered the murderer in a
"swamp" and took him "in irons" to the county jail. Jim himself
tells of his return to Chicago:

> I wa'n't expectin' nothin' in the station, but when we landed
> the whole place was filled back of the gate and I could see that
> they was looking for me. The crowd was about like one that I
> was in down there once when McKinley come to Chicago. A
> squad of policemen came down to meet us, and they got us
> in the middle of the bunch and hurried us into a patrol
> wagon. I could hear the crowd sayin', "That's him; that's the
> murderer; let's lynch him!" "He don't deserve a trial! Let's
> hang him first and then try him!" "The miserable brute!"
> "The contemptible coward!"

Newspapers ran an extra "All 'bout the capture of Jim Jackson."
He was quickly hustled into prison, and with the pressure exerted
by public opinion heated to dangerous fervor, Jim was hurriedly
tried by an obviously antagonistic judge and a highly prejudiced
jury—against which the young, inexperienced court-appointed
lawyer assigned Jackson could do nothing. And while many cases
had prior claim to be heard and had been delayed for two and three
years, Jackson's conviction and sentence were railroaded through
in the minimum time prescribed by due process. Thus on "Friday,

the thirteenth day of this month" Jackson was "to be hanged by the neck till dead." And as Jim finishes his tale, all is ready for the execution. Hank Clery leaves the cell:

> Then Jim got up from his chair and stumbled to the door. "Hank! Hank! S'pose—you—stop at the—telegraph—office—the Western Union—and the—Postal—all of 'em—mebbe—might—be somethin'. . . ." "All right," Hank called back, "I will! I will! I'll go to both to make sure if there's anything there; and I'll telephone you by the time you've got through eatin'."

On this note Darrow concludes *An Eye for An Eye*. Chicago has spawned, raised, conditioned, and now makes ready to destroy with a biological ruthlessness, Jim Jackson, one of its children.

In 1929 when Clarence Darrow delivered his lecture "Facing Life Fearlessly," he quoted in full A. E. Housman's poem "The Culprit," a work which telescopically synthesizes the plight of an unfortunate murderer "in his blindness and terror":

> The night my father got me
>     His mind was not on me;
> He did not plague his fancy
>     To muse if I should be
>     The son you see.
>
> The day my mother bore me
>     She was a fool and glad,
> For all the pain I cost her,
>     That she had borne the lad
>     That borne she had.
>
> My mother and my father
>     Out of the light they lie;
> The warrant would not find them,
>     And here 'tis only I
>     Shall hang on high.
>
> Oh let no man remember
>     The soul that God forgot
> But fetch the county kerchief
>     And noose me in the knot,
>     And I will rot.

> For so the game is ended
> That should not have begun
> My father and my mother
> They have a likely son,
> And I have none.

Grimly appropriate words to the love song of Jim Jackson.

Contemporary notices of *An Eye for An Eye* revealed that critics did not look upon the book as a literary oddity turned out by a lawyer gone wrong; nor was the novel regarded as a screaming polemic that chanted social justice, deplored capital punishment, and decried the basic fallacies in our economic system. The *Independent*, for example, agreed that the book "is one that will hold the reader's interest from cover to cover":

> For the first few pages the reader's heart is hardened against a man who could do so atrocious a deed, whatever the circumstances might be. Gradually, however, as the murderer tells his story to his most intimate friend on the eve of the hanging, the reader's sympathy is aroused. . . . The story is one of life among the poor, where the all-absorbing question is mere existence. The condemned man has had difficulties and discouragements to meet that would take the heart out of the strongest man.

Clarence Darrow's social message apparently was well received by this anonymous reviewer, but more significant was the evaluation given by Grace Isabel Colbron, a critic for the *Bookman*, who realized that the story of Jim Jackson involved something more than a social problem novel about the "submerged tenth" of humanity:

> If to create an illusion, to attain the effect aimed at, completely and entirely, is literary art, then Mr. Darrow's work is literary art of the highest, in spite of an apparent neglect of all the canons of literary art.

*An Eye for An Eye* vigorously crosscuts the traditions in American letters encompassing the strain of Social Darwinism and art; the bitter natural struggle and warfare between the classes, tempered by heroic tragedy and pursuit and questing. The archetypal fall from innocence occurs not in a highly-stylized Garden of Eden, but in a railroad freight yard and in a slum apartment overlooking pushcarts. With movement inside a static philosophic frame and with juxtapositions of material and spiritual poverty, rational beings are forced to work out their destinies from morally perverse and economically irreconcilable postures. With these formulas, Darrow has contributed an artistic expression both of distilled naturalism and real, human drama set against an aesthetic of pessimism and the ever-glamorous backdrop of war.

"Sometimes," moans Jim Jackson, "I think if I hadn't been so poor and in debt I never would have done it, and I don't believe I would." Thus the condemned killer begins to psychologize himself and to reveal to the reader his extreme awareness of the motives and alternatives open to him in his simple quest for the mere necessities of life. He sits in his cell with Clery, drinks "Scotch whiskey" kindly supplied by a sympathetic guard, and talks with a loose tongue:

> Peddlin' is kind of hard work. You got to get up before daylight and go down and get your potatoes and veg't'bles and things, then you have to drive all over and ask everyone to buy, and most people won't take anything from you 'cause you're a peddler and they're 'fraid you'll cheat 'em. . . . And of course, half of the year it's awful hot drivin' 'round the streets and the other half it's awful cold, and sometimes it rains and snows and you get all wet and cold, and it ain't very healthy either. Most peddlers have the consumption, but then there's lots of poor people has consumption.

The self-pitying tone, absent as Jackson went methodically about his day-to-day chores as a street vendor, comes from his attempting now in the shadow of the gallows to universalize his piteous plight and to offer explanation of the human condition that could make a killer out of any individual, however moral and law abiding: "I never intended to kill anybody but somehow everything just led up to it, and I didn't know I was gettin' into it until it was done, and now here I am." Indeed, as early as the time when his wife's red waist aroused in him an erotic urge, Fate began to trigger the mechanism that forecast the eventual catastrophe. Jim Jackson with a tragic perception realizes, at last, how mechanistic forces have conspired against him, have rendered him an impotent agent, and have appointed him to stand as a social sacrifice for a crime he was powerless to avoid committing:

I thought most about that beefsteak, and how I stopped and bought it, and didn't go in and get a drink, and all the time it seemed to me as if that was where I made my big mistake. And then I thought how awful near I came to goin' into the saloon instead of the butchershop. . . . . . . Another thing where I almost missed killin' her was that poker; that coal pail didn't belong in the settin' room at all, but ought to have been in the kitchen, and I don't know how it ever got in there. Mebbe the boy lugged it in for a drum. . . the coal pail was in the settin' room and the poker was in the pail, and they was right before my eyes at the time. If they hadn't been I never would've used the poker.

The biological reaction of animals to stimuli and the harsh coincidences of Fate inexorably spell disaster for Jackson. His wife's red waist; the impulsive gesture to buy a substantial steak rather than to squander fifteen cents on a transient drink; the accidental placing at hand of the murder weapon; the blaring publicity of an anti-crime crusade; and most vital, but least controllable of all, Jackson's volatile nature which completely obliterates at moments of stress his capacity for positive reflective action:

. . . all the time I was thinkin' I could feel a kind of prickin' up in my head, as if a lot of needles was runnin' up toward my hair. I s'pose it was the blood runnin' up there. That feller that I told you about that was talkin' to us over here kind of made out that a man was a good deal like a machine, or an engine of some kind, and when the steam was turned on he had to go. He said that if the blood was pumped up in the head it made us do things; it made some people write poetry, and some make speeches, and some sing, and some fight, and some kill folks and they couldn't really help it if they was made that way and the blood got pumped up in the head. I believe there's a good deal in it.

And so when Jim and his aroused spouse verbally flay each other, he recalls that "by this time I had a prickly feelin' runnin' all through my head and up into my hair, and I didn't really think of anything. . . ." The forces which had set these waves of circumstance in motion refuse to be halted. Jackson sorrowfully confesses: "If ther'd been forty scaffolds right before my eyes I'd have brought down that poker just the same."

Darrow gives movement to the suspenseful drama when Jim narrates the tale of his eerie ride across the prairie with the corpse of his wife bundled in the rear of the wagon. The chaotic psychology of Jackson nearly drives him to the breaking point as he makes his feeble, foolish, bumbling attempt to dispose of the body. The night is freezing and snowy as he begins his journey to the flats, passing through various "rough" neighborhoods and even being stopped once by a gang of rowdies who called themselves the "Bridgeport Threshers." He passes a policeman who regards the wagon with some suspicion but does nothing; he passes noisy saloons, and on the road Jackson encounters "lots of wagons" with people out riding for mere pleasure or returning from parties: "I never had no idea how many people traveled nights before," Jackson perplexedly observes, realizing suddenly the barren despair that has characterized his lot in life. There are joy riders every night; his first nocturnal trip, however, is not, to say the least, one of pleasure and amusement. As his spavined mare shambles along the snow-covered, mud-crusted road, Jim begins to behave like a character creation of Poe:

> After a while I begun to have a queer idea about her [his wife]. I thought I could feel her lookin' right at me—kind of feel her eyes. I drove on, and said it was all bosh and she couldn't do it, and I looked down at her feet and I seen they was in the same place, but still I couldn't get over that feelin'. I thought she was lookin' at me all the time, and I kind of 'magined I could hear her say, "Where 're you takin' me? Where 're you takin' me?" just about the same as when she said, "Kill me! Kill me! Kill me!" and no matter what I done, or how hard I tried, I could feel her lookin' and hear them words in my ears.

As the murderer continues his journey and the surroundings become more isolated, the tension within Jackson rises and his panic continues to increase:

> Then I kept hearin' them words plainer than I had before. . . . Then I began to think of the things I'd read about people who were dead . . . about people that were put away for dead, when they wa'n't dead at all, and about mesmerism and hypnotism, and Christian Science, but I knew none of them things was done the way she'd been killed. Then I re-

membered about trances, and how people was give up for dead . . . and even buried and then come to life, and about how people had dug up old graveyards and found out where lots of people had moved around after they's dead.

His disordered mind unhinged by panic, Jackson reverts to primitive instincts of unreason and superstition, the genesis of atavism engulfing his entire personality until with a strength born of this dense fear, he believes that his wife still lives. He must see her:

I couldn't stand it any more, and I looked at her feet, but they hadn't moved, and then I stopped the horse and got off'n the wagon and went back to the hind end and lifted up the blanket kind of slow. For I felt as if I'd stand more chance that way than if I did it all at once, and I got the blanket up, and then I got hold of the quilt just by the edges and kind of pulled it back so as to uncover her face, and just then the moon came out from behind a cloud and shone right down in her face, almost like day, and she looked just as white as a ghost, and the bandage had come off her jaw and it hung clear down, and her mouth was open, and I knew she was dead.

Now Jackson, restored to comparative sanity, can finish the deed, satisfied that no spirit manifestations are operating their mysterious spells as revenge against an evil doer and social profaner.

In the South Jim finds that the Negroes are his most compatible acquaintances: "I always liked to talk with the niggers; they never asked me any questions, and I never was 'fraid that they'd been in Chicago, and I didn't really think they took any of the papers, for they didn't know how to read." His identification with the Negroes becomes exceedingly close; working at charcoal pits, Jackson and his partner become so dirty that they can not be distinguished "from darkies." And in his flight through Mississippi as Jim begs food at the countryside shanties in the backwoods an "old darkey lady" gives him some food: ". . . and as I sat and et it . . . . a whole lot of woolly-headed pickaninnies sat and looked at me every mouthful. One of 'em was about the size of my kid, and made me think of him a good deal. . . ." The pursued can relax only in the company of the Negroes, for at other times he warily guards against revealing anything of his past and he constantly tussles with wild nightmares which Darrow has constructed, interestingly, not out of Spencer, but out of Freud:

> I run to a little stream and follered it up same as I used to read in Indian stories. . . . And I kind of saw her face, and she seemed to be follerin' me too, only she didn't seem to have any legs or much of anything, except just her face and a kind of long white train . . . and she always seemed to know just the right place no matter how careful I hid. . . .

After so emotional a drain-contending with hounds, apparitions, and the imminence of capture at any moment, Jackson awakens from this traumatic vision, sees "a darkey there in the barn feedin' a mule." The Negro said, " 'Hello, boss!' just as friendly, and asked me where I was going." Again Jackson finds peace and relaxation by a relationship, no matter how peripheral, with a Negro. Indeed, when a prospective employer asked Jim if he minded "workin' with niggers," Jim declares, "I told him I didn't care anything 'bout that; I guessed they was as good as I was." Such an attitude emanating from one of the inhabitants of "the lower depths" was in direct contrast to the caricatures presented to habitues of the vaudeville stage of the times. Jackson was transcending the philosophy of his status. His subsequent capture by the mercenary law enforcement officials is brought about by a white lady's refusal to give the begging vagrant some food.

Through all his misadventures, however, Jackson perceives the essential disaster that is constantly stalking him, and this basic tragedy of perception is alleviated only by the protagonist's strong desire to live, even in the face of the impossible forces he can never combat, much less defeat. Jim, indeed, is more than an adequate forerunner of Clyde Griffiths, whose guileless fall from innocence reflected for Theodore Dreiser the stark essentials of an American tragedy. Both protagonists were driven by the unseen forces in this "rudderless universe" to irrational—criminal, in the view of society —acts. Now society as a whole, responsible as a sinful collaborator for their actions, must be avenged, and Clarence Darrow's major character, with his ugly, sophisticated wisdom, manifests his sensitive realization of what Nathaniel Hawthorne's Parson Hooper of "The Minister's Black Veil" tried to illustrate personally for his suspicious and frightened congregation of visible saints: that on every visage is a black veil, that all mankind is figuratively bound in a mammoth brotherhood of sin and guilt. At the same time, irrational, inconspicuous, insignificant man is completely powerless when caught in the systematic crossfire of Nature's most hostile forces; lacking personal agency he is marked as if by Election for his doom. As in the fierce biological process of struggle and survival, justice and mercy are lacking in our collaborative phenomenon of Society; the temporal arm of authority necessarily erects uncompromising moral laws to preserve the oligarchic mould in which mechanistic forces must continue to operate again and again.

*An Eye for An Eye*, then, is not merely a piece of tractarian propaganda; though essentially unified it is not "tragedy" in the Greek sense of the term; it is, however, a potent slice of formularized Darwinism that is superimposed over a contemporary social  battlefield of spectacular notoriety: the "Bandit's Roost" as photographed by Jacob A. Riis and the urban slum neighborhoods as depicted by the Ash-Can School of painters. Darrow's hero, ignoble in the extreme, is finally buffeted into submission by the incessant narrowing of his field of vision and final reduction of his free choice to naught. When man cannot gratify his most necessary drives through socially acceptable means, he is then forced by the animalism inherent in everyone to transgress the mores. The book truthfully serves "as a receptacle for Darrow's ideas on poverty, social justice, crime and the revenge motive under which society executes those who have been driven to take a human life"; it is also one of the early novels "in American literature to deal with the life of the poor, with their hard incessant labors, debts, fears and want." Darrow's writing is coarse and crude; while his ear for the parlance of the gutter is good, his ability to make it a colorful addition to the novel is weak. But in its rugged, bludgeoning tone lies the powerful totality of effect in the work. The single emotional overtone emphasized throughout *An Eye for An Eye* is fear, and every line and intonation are directed toward this particular end: fear for economic disaster that would obliterate a family group; fear of supernatural, mystical forces of the unknown; fear for personal safety; and the underwritten, nevertheless awesome, fear of death. This singleness of artistic purpose, this basic unity of emotional design, Darrow fits perfectly into the unpolished machinery of his novel. One adulatory critic calls this book "one of the few earliest examples of American realistic writing . . ." and "the forerunner of the Chicago realistic school which flourished during the 1920's." Although both of these assertions contain some extravagance, *An Eye for An Eye* is indeed something more than emotional overflow or unreflective literary frenzy. The book, a combined vehicle for art and thought, embodies, in the final analysis, the philosophic seeds which, by the 1920's, had led Darrow to shift his hypothesis regarding Non-Resistance, vengeance, and evil. He had come to lose his Utopian belief in the essential perfectability of the race: man was not Rousseau's epitome of noble splendor; rather he was the incarnate beast described by Thomas Hobbes as a "wolf." The innate evil of man's chemistry, then, taught Darrow the inadequacy of self-sacrifice and the futility of belief in heavenly justice for mortals. Herman Melville in *Pierre, or The Ambiguities* (1852) metaphorically asserted that "a virtuous expediency . . . seems the highest desirable or attainable earthly excellence for the mass of men" for "in things terrestrial . . . a man must not be governed by ideas celestial. . . ." Furthermore,

> When they [men] go to heaven, it will be quite another thing. There, they can freely turn the left cheek, because there the right cheek will never be smitten. There they can freely give all to the poor, for *there* there will be no poor to give to.

Pierre Glendinning, his life dominated by a calculated pursuit of highest moral and ethical values, eventually comes to regard himself as "the fool of Truth, the fool of Virtue, and the Fool of Fate." Clarence Darrow would concur in this evaluation of a life foolishly spent. One must synchronize his moral frequency by the impulses of earth rather than heaven. The attorney had learned too well the fate of those in the slums and ghettos of Chicago who, governed momentarily by an admirable religious inpulse, had once turned the other cheek.

## Chapter 5

# IN THE MIDST OF LIFE

WHEN Clarence Darrow concluded his summation in The Kidd Case on the last day of October, 1898, he revealed some autobiographical phenomena that formed in part his intellect and character:

> I happen to have been born of an Abolition father and mother, back in the Western Reserve of Ohio, one of the stations of the underground railroad in those early days, when it was a crime to take a poor Negro and send him on his way to liberty and light. . . . I was born under these circumstances and conditions, and I well remember when scarce a babe . . . I heard my people tell of those brave men and women, Garrison, Kelley, Foster, Pillsbury and others of their kind who took their fortunes, their lives and their reputations in their hands, who traveled up and down the land the best they could, preaching their doctrines to all who would stop and hear. They were criminals, they were outlaws . . . but those outlaws, those disreputables, those men and women spurned, despised and accused, were the forerunners of a brighter and more glorious day. . . .

Indeed, while Darrow's experience with reformers, trade unionists, legislators, and other prominent contemporaries brought a degree of intellectual and social nourishment to the attorney, so also was he forever a product of the Western Reserve of Ohio, an integral part of its philosophical heritage and, at the same time, its spiritual dilemmas. Especially in his literary ambitions and artistic desires did remembrances of northeastern Ohio purvey for Clarence Darrow images of his initiation into life itself. Paradoxically, he produced nothing there as a writer; as a lawyer, his most important case in Ashtabula had involved "an action of replevin for a harness worth fifteen dollars." Yet the imprint of the area upon Darrow transcends by far the ordinary sentimentalism evoked in anyone by hazy recollections of a somewhat happy life during the good years of youth. Always an astute observer and keen dissector of the social situation, Darrow, early in the literary impulse of his career decided to focus his talent upon life and action in the Middle West community as he recalled it.

By 1903 the growing mass of Darrow's admirers were beseeching their champion to announce his candidacy for Chicago's mayorality race. Old friends of the Sunset Club and the Henry George Club along with the labor unionists and proletarians who had gloried in the counsellor's defenses of Gene Debs and Big Bill Haywood, were captivated by the courtroom oratory of this man who was coming to symbolize muscular non-conformity; even this early Darrow was rapidly becoming "one of the most fascinating men America has ever produced." It was on a European tour in 1903 that the vacationing lawyer, "plying his pencil like lightning over his paper," wrote *Farmington*, a novel centering about a boyhood and youth in the area of northeastern Ohio and revealing a grotesque idyl of persons hopelessly warped by environment. While Clarence Darrow was innocence abroad "looking out at the Matterhorn" or sightseeing in Geneva, he was not the contemporary stereotype of the businesslike, culture-hungry American tourist, but a sensitive novelist laying open the emotional and spiritual vitals of middlewestern villagers. The novel was published in 1904, and despite his booming reputation as a legal genius and crusader for the underdog, little fanfare surrounded the appearance of *Farmington*. Today, more than half a century later, few have heard of it; even fewer have read it. From its very publication, Darrow's novel of revolt against the village seemed unfortunately augured for obscurity. While the cult of Darrow enthusiasts and admirers saw *Farmington* through small printings by McClurg, Huebsch, Liveright, and Scribner's, an accurate assessment would be Charles Yale Harrison's: *Farmington* has had "an even drawn out success" but not the recognition it fully deserves.

The initial neglect of *Farmington* is not at all difficult to understand. Most "ordinary" readers in 1904 were excited by the violence perpetrated by Nietzschean superman Wolf Larson in Jack London's widely publicized *The Sea Wolf* or charmed by the buoyant spirits of Gene Stratton Porter's winsome *Freckles*, whose title character was described as "a plucky waif who guards the Limberlost timber leases and dreams of Angels." Each of these novels sold more than 750,000 copies. Best-seller lists across the nation in 1904 advertised the metropolitan journalese of O. Henry (*Cabbages and Kings*), the historical panorama of Winston Churchill (*The Crossing*), and the romantic fantasy of George Barr McCutcheon (*Beverly of Graustark*.) Intellectuals of the day were puzzling over Henry James's latest, *The Golden Bowl,* or interpreting the speculative hypothesis set forth by Henry Adams in his privately-printed *Mont St. Michel,* while the righteous indignation of muckraking enthusiasts was aroused to a fever by Lincoln Steffens' blockbuster, *The Shame of the Cities.* The little publicized appearance of *Farmington,* then, a work from the hand of a semiprofessional writer, caused faint stir among such imposing competition. Darrow was a neophyte novelist whose sketch book was critically nullified by the impressive reputations and talents of more professional authors who had long since discovered the literary techniques leading to the rewards of contemporary recognition.

In addition *Farmington* was hurt by contemporary reviewers who were unable to perceive that Clarence Darrow had not skirted the surface of life but had written a highly complex, suggestive novel of terrifying psychological proportions. Darrow unfortunately was presented either as a facile recorder of childhood nostalgia or as a complacent appreciator of the beauties of rural life. While these flimsy designations probably led many a genteel reader to buy the book, the sub-literary scrap heap was then rapidly growing with sentimental volumes picturing the great outdoors and, in the phrase of incumbent President Theodore Roosevelt, the strenuous life. As this *genrè* faded into critical disrespect, Darrow's misread novel sank beneath notice of the literary scene's most reputable commentators. The "keynote of *Farmington,*" wrote an anonymous magazine reviewer, "is the misunderstanding of childhood by grown-ups and the constant antagonism of children to their elders." Further, the critic noted:

> "It is just like Huck Finn," was the comment on the book by a twelve year old boy, and, in fact, the same antagonism that characterizes Mark Twain's immortal little ne'er-do-well is visible in this well-cared-for son of worthy parents.

The elegant picture of an impish Little Lord Fauntleroy, a rage then in process of slow decline, was presented also by Wilbur C. F.

Wright, reviewer for the *Nation*, who called *Farmington* "An idyl
not complex nor [sic] psychological" with the "picture" being
"charming enough" on "its lighter side":

> But it is obvious that what strikes him [Darrow] with most
> force . . . is the lack of knowledge of the childish mind, the
> lack of sympathy with childish pains and pleasures that most
> children have to endure from their elders.

Most reviewers of the day eulogized Darrow's rural episodes in
terms connoting the freshness and vigor of episodes from *Boy's
Life*. In its unhappy contemporary reception, *Farmington* was considered as being within the established formula of a current literary fashion.

One modern critic accurately places *Farmington* as an early illustration of the "revolt from the village" in American letters, but
other current appraisals lead in no way to a proper perspective of
this literary enigma. Darrow's biographer asserts that "artistic
symmetry and perfection" are most evident in the attorney's
"American classic." Friends of Darrow, hopelessly blinded by their
adulation of the man, point out his "poetic rhythms" and his
"genius for the precise phrase." The artistry of *Farmington*, however, does not lie in the delicate shadings and hues observed by
some idolatrous critics; nor does it manifest itself in an idyllic
reverie extolling the plantation at sundown or the old swimmin'
hole. The artistic success of Clarence Darrow in this novel derives
from the fully charged blunderbuss he levelled at a sterile, in-
sensate community staggering like a drunken man and encroaching
upon the private conscience of its inhabitants. Darrow incorporated
into his book the Darwinist principles he had been perfecting in
his thought, along with the stylistic brand of stolid, careful realism in the tradition developed and publicized by his friend
Howells. The artful analysis of the Buckeye personality in terms
social and psychological establish *Farmington* as a forerunner both
of Anderson's *Winesburg, Ohio* and of a major neglected American novel, Brand Whitlock's *J. Hardin & Son*—books which
erupted in the early 'twenties and drew attention to the anti-village
school, whose celebrated leaders Sinclair Lewis and Zona Gale
penned major contributions (*Main Street* and *Faint Perfume*) to
establish the popularity of this thematic concern. The novel which

Clarence Darrow composed in Europe, then, anticipated by nearly fifteen years the spate of Midwest anti-village manifestoes and outlined in the author's economical sketches of the town and its people an idea that soon came coursing through the very mainstream of contemporary American letters. Here was a lawyer not only interested in writing about crime and criminals. Clarence Darrow in *Farmington* made a serious bid to alter the image America had developed of him. He yearned to be considered as a reflective artist whose creative intellect and talent lay not only in but also beyond the area of courts and prisons. *Farmington* was his attempt to establish this public impression of himself.

Darrow's novel, as American an Odyssey as the river journey of Huck Finn, is, like the Twain classic, picaresque. John Smith, the middle-aged narrator, from his mature vantage point offers sundry autobiographical recollections of his childhood, youth, and young manhood in a hypothetical village called Farmington. Smith, the central figure in a series of flashbacks, possesses excellent recall for careful details geographical, educational, and genealogical. He is able to present with colorful accuracy various slices of life in his town as observed through the eyes of an extremely sensitive youngster whose incisively remembered perceptions are now given more depth and meaning by the narrator's polish and sophistication. The twenty-three chapters of *Farmington*, then, have no plot in the conventional connotation of the term; there is generated no specific conflict that pits in human terms protagonist and antagonist; there is no climax; no tensions are built to a resolution. Truthfully, one who reads Darrow's novel carelessly might be tempted, as were some reviewers, to classify it with William Dean Howells' *A Boy's Town* (1890) or Mrs. Harriet Beecher Stowe's *Old Town Folks* (1869). There are moments of the "boyhood idyl" and there are occasional, quaint sketches of "just plain folks" in a small town. When Sara Andrew Shafer of the *Dial* noted in an essay titled "Through the Eyes of a Boy" that *Farmington* "is a book for boys, for women—but above all, it is a book for men who have once been boys. . . . It is not a book for the limited express, or the smoking room of an inn," she had in mind only certain portions of the novel containing brief sections on some of the more romantic aspects of youth. "The District School," "The Sunday School," "About Girls," "Holidays," "Baseball," indeed, are chapters with the materials of uncritical reminiscence about them. But close scrutiny soon reveals that John Smith does not possess the peripheral observations one might expect of writer intent on portraying a pastoral scene of the long ago, but the retrospective qualities and insights of a mature iconoclast focusing his animus on various aspects of life in the rural Middlewest as it was during the disjointed ante-bellum and post-Civil War days. Citizens in fictional Spoon River, Illinois; Gopher Prairie, Minnesota; and Winesburg and Macochee (Brand Whitlock's wasteland), Ohio, would have discovered numerous counterparts already populating the village of Farmington.

John Smith wandered and blundered "in a zigzag path through childhood within the narrow shadow of the stubborn little town" which ordered and oriented the destinies of all its people. Quickly introduced into the real world "of selfishness and greed," the young man was, at the conclusion of his spiritual apprenticeship, initiated into the life of passive despair led by his fellow townsfolk:

> All my life [Smith records] I have been planning and hoping and thinking and dreaming and loitering and waiting. All my life I have been getting ready to begin to do something, something worth the while. I have been waiting for the summer and waiting for the fall; I have been waiting for the winter and waiting for the spring; waiting for the night and waiting for the morning; waiting and dawdling and dreaming, until the day is almost spent and the twilight close at hand.

A real product of Farmington—inanimate prototype of the mechanistic tyrant and all-consuming Force that appeared under various guises (railroads, packing-houses, factories) in the works of late nineteenth century American authors—John Smith is rendered fit to join the peculiar company of T. S. Eliot's modern symbol for emotional impotency and intellectual indecision, J. Alfred Prufrock, whose sterile complacent existence of passivity and acceptance at last stripped him of his ability to act. Smith, too, is cut from the same pattern as Henry James's John Marcher, who in "The Beast in the Jungle" fruitlessly waited for the singular cataclysmic event that he felt would alter in dramatic fashion the course of his personal destiny and fulfill the great void in his thin, nerveless life. Yet Smith feels that resistance against the Fates is useless, for he resolutely believes that Farmington village, with unadorned hostility, directs the flow of life within its corporate limits: "It took years of care and toil," he muses, "to show me that life is stronger than man, that conditions control individuals." This theory of human irresponsibility, then, becomes intertwined with the obvious Darwinist implications of struggle and survival that turns humans into fierce Hobbesian wolves: even the children in school "were young savages, always grasping for the best, ever fighting and scheming to get the advantage." And in the background Farmington remains placid and serene as its natural beauty is superimposed over a throbbing vortex of provincial orthodoxy and Neo-Puritanism in all matters of the mind and the spirit. The degenerative force that symbolizes the existence of middlewestern villages becomes the major theme of John Smith, the wickedly perceptive outspoken skeptic, as he endeavors to reveal the magnetic chain of disillusion that binds into a sinful microcosm inhabitants of the narrator's stunted village.

*Farmington* presents also the humdrum and static conditions that nearly drove Carol Kennicott insane on the Main Street of Gopher Prairie: education in the village: "Whipping was a part, and a large part of the regular course . . . ; religion in Farmington, "a very Godly place": "the church seemed to have been built to accommodate all the people in the world and then have room to spare"; business in Farmington: "cunning soulless farmers . . . dickered and haggled about [the miller's] hard-earned toll"; recreation in Farmington: "I saw the cruel boy push the barbed hook through the whole length of the squirming worm. . . . In a short time he pulled out a wiggling little fish . . . stuck a willow twig through its bleeding gills and strung it on a stick"; ambition in Farmington: ". . . day after day and year after year he was compelled to walk the short and narrow path between the little house and the decaying mill, while his mind was roving over scenes of great battles, decayed empires, dead languages, and the starry heavens above. To his dying day he lived in a walking trance . . ." These kaleidoscopic truisms of the town, its activities, and its pulse, however, act only as corollaries to the major dissection at hand. *Farmington*, mainly, deals with "life and action, and boys and girls, and men and women . . ."—people to whom Smith refers as "the weird fantastic troop that pushed themselves before my pencil." Most of all the novel involves a series of close character analyses which reveal for the modern reader a book of the grotesque analyzing Neo-Puritanism among the Buckeyes. The *dramatis personae* of this loose record includes *isolatoes* who have come to the point of embracing one single truth to live by and who in making this particular truth a living ethic warp their entire beings: "life is mostly illusions, and the illusions of infancy and childhood and youth are more alluring than those of later years." "Each truth," as Sherwood Anderson was to write later in *Winesburg, Ohio,* "was a composite of a great many vague thoughts. All about in the world were the truths and they were all beautiful." Clarence Darrow through his eloquent narrator presents a series of Farmingtonians all in search of the real values that are never devastated; a search that characterizes those maimed souls haunted and harassed by countless pressures, fears, and superstitions; a search fruitless in the spiritually barren environment of the arc Smith has circumscribed for his actors.

Ferman Henry, the local carpenter, was, in the language of the village, "a very shiftless man." He lived with his large family in a wooden slum whose "clapboards had begun to brown with age and wind and rain" and whose general decrepitude stood as constant irritant to respectable Farmington. Although Henry was a "good" carpenter, he conscientiously dodged work and never completed a job once undertaken, not even necessary repairs to finish his own house. The people of the village, puzzled by the erratic behavior of this man, held as intrinsic to their philosophy "that everyone should not only work, but also like to work simply for the pleasure it brought." Indeed, the colorless tedium of workaday routine, they felt, isolated man from and insulated him against the frivolousness of life and the temptations of Satan, who, as their New England ancestors believed, is forever nearby contending with the Almighty for the possession of individual souls. Thus Ferman Henry stood as anathema to the frontier Neo-Puritan who concurred with his forbears of Bay Colony covenant and synod in maintaining that ultimate judgment with the "Sheep" rather than with the "Goats" could be realized through the assiduous discharge of secular duties; furthermore, moral and ethical necessities must be observed, as R. H. Tawney has written, especially when such duties no longer

are material necessities. As a youth Smith and his friends were
told that

> Ferman Henry was too shiftless and lazy ever to complete his
> house, and warned us by his example. When we left our task
> undone, or made excuses for our idleness, they asked us if we
> wanted to grow up as shiftless and lazy as Ferman Henry.

Further indicting Henry for his easy indifference to life was his
idiosyncrasy, as the village regarded it, for attending circuses.
However poor the family was, the entire clan would travel to
town to see any circus that made its way to Farmington: "The
richest people in the village had never been to as many circuses
as the Henry boys. . . ." More than a mere curiosity, however,
Ferman Henry's rejection of Farmington and his acceptance of
carnival and sideshow rigamarole as durable values comprise bit-
ing comments on the schema of the life of his village, for Henry
achieved personal salvation and psychic independence by deliberately relinquishing his place among the local saints. In the exuber-
ance and vitality of the circus this unhappy carpenter discovered
emotional overtones of strength and freedom that he had found
missing in the spiritual structure of his neighbors. This conviction
Ferman Henry embraced as his truth—the grotesquerie that took
this complex character of many dimensions and reduced him, in
the eyes of Farmington, to a stick figure living by a dream ethic
of lion tamers and bare-back riders. The hours at the circus passed
very quickly and as the tent was collapsed, Henry's town, shorn
of its temporary gaiety and spangles, sank into its usual doze.
Life had left Farmington a still point on the pivotal axis of time.
John Smith, much later, returned to visit Ferman Henry:

> The years had slipped over him like days or weeks, and
> scarcely left a furrow on his face or whitened a single hair.

Smith saw Henry's "laughing" grandchildren frolicking in the
yard of the still unfinished house and subsequently "fell to musing
as to who was the wiser—he or I." Henry had lived by the circus
rather than by the Scripture as interpreted by the visible saints.
In this strength of conviction, the narrator feels, lies the ultimate
salvation of his village. Only in the doggedness of a Ferman

Henry resides a living, symbolic affront which can eventually expand the intellectual horizons and spiritual limits of those who discriminate against him and others who reject the Neo-Puritan values imposed by the town. On this paradox, unpalatable to the Farmington mind, Smith rests the dubious future of his boyhood home.

Aunt Mary, one of the local gentlefolk, lived, as a contemporary reviewer noted, "in bondage to a heartless idol called Neatness." Actually, the plight of this unfortunate reveals with a quiet poignancy how completely inter-personal communication had broken down in the village. For many years this pathetic old lady had been planning a party to which all the very best of local society would come. In her mansion Aunt Mary had set aside a special room for this projected affair: no one was allowed to enter the sanctified parlor which was impeccably furnished far beyond her means with a "real Brussels carpet with big red and black flower figures" on the floor; "the entire room was without blemish or spot." Indeed, "the house was always white, as if freshly painted the day before." This "disease," this "ruling passion of her life," as Smith calls it, was most evident in the drawing room which once she had shown Smith "with all the pride of possession and detail of description of a lackey who shows wandering Americans the belongings of an old English castle or country seat." The supreme elegance of Aunt Mary's creative powers was realized in the symmetry of her decor, with "cane seated chairs" placed against the different walls which sported "two or three yarn mottoes in black walnut frames . . . and some chromos"; near the center of the room "was a real marble-top table, with a great Bible and a red plush album in the middle." The decorations were completed with a portrait of Aunt Mary's mother and a crayon portrait of her father, "a once famous preacher." Most important to this lady was the fact that in her party room were no flies, the little emblems of decay and germs.

The trappings were ideal, but Aunt Mary's long-anticipated party was never given. Postponed for more than a quarter of a century, the event now achieved reality alone in Mary's mind. Her party room literally was without life of any sort, and symptomatic of Farmington's illness was the dilemma faced by this unhappy woman. Suffering from a severe emotional paralysis that made the dream of the party more meaningful to her than the real thing, she could not bring herself to destroy the pattern of lifelessness that had been built up over the years by the symbolic room. Aunt Mary was incapable of revolting against those principles that motivated Ferman Henry's scrupulous devotion to the circus and its frivolity; the idea of a party and its happy connotations wilted in the presence of the "great Bible" on the "marble-top table" in her party room. Mary was plainly suffocated by the Puritan spirit that pervaded her being and involved, as H. L. Mencken and George Jean Nathan once noted, "the haunting fear that someone, somewhere, may be happy." The vicarious thought was as close to severing the moral straitjacket of Farmington's Neo-Puritanism as Aunt Mary could come. Ferman Henry was able to achieve salvation through his dedicated abuse of the ethic which engulfed his community; through the submission of her being, Aunt Mary was annihilated. Ironically, on the day of Mary's funeral the mourning townspeople tracked mud all over the fine Brussels carpet, and black swarms of midsummer flies covered in diseased-looking patches the immaculate whiteness of her party room. Smith offers the final observation:

> Slowly I looked at the muddy floor, the swarming flies, and the people gathered in Aunt Mary's parlor; and then I thought of the party that she had told me she was going to give.

During the obsequies when the preacher referred to Aunt Mary's "neatness," Uncle Ezra, her husband, was heard to groan; but his deceased wife, if rewarded according to her devotion and subscription to the ethic which embalmed Farmington, passed from visible to invisible sainthood.

Aunt Louisa, a "widow woman," was "old . . . had reddish false hair . . . was fat . . . took snuff . . . talked a great deal . . . belonged to the United Presbyterian Church . . . and sat in a pew clear up in front." Since the death of her husband, Louisa said "that she had no consolation but her religion." Actually Louisa was the moral watchdog of the village whose sacred duty it was, as self-appointed archangel, to cry out against those sinners and disturbers of the Elect who were most avid in their devotion to Satan. Once instigated by this moral incendiary, the village saints set out to purge Farmington of all the devil's votaries. Smith recalled clearly and with shame one debauch in which he had a hand. Aunt Louisa had been "especially interested in some man who lived alone in the village and who had done something terrible"; she felt that "if the men had any spirit they would go there some night and rotten-egg him and ride him on a rail and drum him out of town." Darrow's narrator then tells of the proceedings a few nights later:

> About midnight my brother and I got up and went to the public square. Twenty or thirty men and boys had gathered at the flag-pole. I did not know all their names, but I knew there were some of the best people in the place. I am certain I saw Deacon Cole, and I know that we went over to Squire Allen's carriage-house and got a large plank which he had told the crowd they might have. The men had sticks and stones and eggs, and we all went to the man's house. When we reached the fence, we opened the gate and went inside and began throwing stones and sticks at the house and through the windows; and we broke in the front door with Squire Allen's plank. All the men and boys hooted and jeered with the greatest glee. I can still remember seeing a half-dressed man run out of the back door of the house, down the garden path, and get away. I can never forget his scared white face as he passed me in the gloom. After breaking all the doors and windows, we went home and went to bed, thinking we had done something brave and noble, and helped the morals of the town.

On the following day "little knots of people" gathered about town to talk about the "raid." Only a few people spoke out against what had been done; but these faint dissenters, Smith remembers, were "by no means the best citizens."

As the motivating force behind this purgative orgy, Aunt Louisa felt that she derived, as had the Puritan stewards, holy authority directly from the Almighty and that any righteous act of retribution was taken justifiably in His name. Thus this pious Farmington widow possessed a spirit suffused with the Bay Colony ethic: the militant orthodoxy of an Endicott, the hell-fire hysteria of fearful New England maidens, and the peerless, holy virtue of the Salem (1692) Magistrates. In the Farmington of John Smith's youth she found status and direction for her inflammatory talent. When the evil doer had been driven from the village

Aunt Louisa was radiant. She made her tour of the neighborhood and told how she approved of the bravery of the men
and boys. She said that everyone after this would know that
Farmington was a moral town.

Aunt Louisa's truth, then, differs in shading from the truths of
Ferman Henry and Aunt Mary; yet the three remain embodiments
of all the grotesques in the town: those who revolt, those who rebel
in spirit but who conform in mind, and those who accept with a
wholehearted fanaticism the values imposed on their individual
personalities. Of this last type is Aunt Louisa, at whose death "the
whole town was in mourning." The good lady was given "a beautiful funeral," so her friends told, and "in a few months a fine monument was placed on the little lot"—this out of gratitude for her
faithful dedication to the virtue and the purity of the town. The
"hunted man" who had been driven from Farmington by Louisa's
hosts "died a year or so afterwards." Someone "bought him a
lonely grave on the outskirts of the churchyard where he could not
harm anyone who lay slumbering there."
  Not the least significant character in *Farmington* is the narrator's
father, a miller transplanted from New England, who had been
"raised in the Puritan school of life." Now in his new surroundings
he withdrew from the church and became regarded as the village
infidel. A misfit in the town because he loved "study and con-
templation," the miller was a social pariah whose presence among
the saints was as offensive as the circulation of a Colonel Ingersoll
treatise on morals. This voracious and intelligent reader and
dreamer was now surrounded by countless antagonisns that threatened to erupt into permanent hostility. As his son records

  A strange fate had set him down beside the little winding
  creek and kept him at his humble task of tolling his neighbors' grist. He looked at the high hills to the east, and the
  high hills to the west, and up and down the narrow country
  road that led to the outside world. He knew that beyond the
  high hills was a broad inviting plain, with opportunity and
  plenty, with fortune and fame; but as he looked at the hills
  he could see no way to pass beyond. It is possible that he
  could have walked over them, or even around them, had he
  been alone; but there was the ever-growing brood that held

him in the narrow place. No doubt as he grew older he often looked up and down the long dusty road, half expecting some fairy or genie to come along and take him away where he might realize his dreams; but of course no such thing ever happened—for this is a real story—and so he stayed and ground the grain in the old decaying mill.

The world of "reverie" and "the world in which he lives" are in constant conflict for the patient, scholarly-inclined miller—a man whose dreams never rose beyond the village limits, so thoroughly were they ravaged by Farmington. "All my life," states Smith, "I have felt that Nature had some grudge against my father," for "the fairy-lands of which his old volumes told" could never, however blurred and distorted, be brought into any focus with the existence now imposed upon him. As "the chain grew stronger" the ageing miller began looking to his children "to satisfy the dreams that life once held out to him"; throughout his lifetime he was, as his son relates, "a simple child . . . from the time when he first saw the light until his friends and comrades lowered him into the sandy loam of the old churchyard." The local heathen, frustrated by his surroundings, adhered to that truth of integrity wherein his strong spiritual resources more than compensated for his paucity of material wealth. Always to question orthodoxy of any sort, Smith senior was emotionally brutalized unthinkingly and ruthlessly by the reeling community of Elect about him. His solace lay in the Emersonian apothegm, that for nonconformity "the world whips you with its displeasure."

The miscellany of grotesques with which Clarence Darrow peopled his first novel is indeed considerable. Analyses of other Farmingtonians who flit in and out of the tale intensify the impression made on the narrator by the local citizenry with whom he had spent so many years: Deacon Cole, whose life was one trite proverb after another; Squire Allen, whose majesty and bearing symbolized for his neighbors the grandeur and regality of the Holy Roman Empire; Henry Pitkin, whose sickly, tender features and pious demeanor gave rise to many a rumor among the Sunday School classes he taught—all had their demons. All were germs in the contagion that was Farmington, a town where damaged souls suffered from qualms of the spirit that transcended merely peripheral problems of adjustment and acceptance. These people created by

Clarence Darrow were not plodding theories, wearily struggling from page to page; nor are they familiar stereotypes with singular astonishing aberrations. The lawyer breathed reality and depth into people who were possessed with problems which legislation alone, unfortunately, could not help: those humans who are silently, nonetheless inevitably, crushed. In the preface to the second edition of *Farmington* Clarence Darrow answered a question which had been put to him by nearly everyone who read the book: Are John Smith, the narrator, and Clarence Darrow, the attorney, one and the same? His answer: ". . . no one can sincerely write of any but himself, or feel any emotions but his own." Darrow, indeed, admirably set down with feeling and acuteness his description of and his indictment against the village. An education in failure was the lot of John Smith, who, having at length risen above his early environment through native, natural endowments, now returns to the battleground he had known—the field on which he was transformed from uninitiated rookie to scarred, knowing veteran. The education was hard but the narrator was fortunate to derive at least one valuable lesson: "It is only our mistakes and failures and trials and sins that teach how really alike are all human souls, and how strong is the fate that overrides all earthly schemes."

Darrow built in *Farmington* a literary absolute as succinct as Melville's *Pequod*, as controversial as Roger Williams's vessel of toleration, as navigable as Huck Finn's raft, as American as Longfellow's ship of state. The demons polluting the town and its people are carefully scrutinized within the limits of the mechanistic philosophy the lawyer had circumscribed about his thought: man is a machine emotionally stimulated by Hobbesian viciousness; "man is a little more complex organism than an amoeba . . . [but] there isn't so much difference at that"; man reacts to the most elemental tropisms on an earth that is "one of the most insignificant spots of mud in the whole untraversed universe." Indeed Clarence Darrow recognized, but never softened, the relentlessness of his theoretic stance:

> I am not here to give you any consolation. I am not going to give you any consolation excepting this, that in a world of egotistic people who have nothing to brag about excepting their ignorance, a frame that is capable of some joy but of much pain, and whose constant accompaniment is pain, in a

world of that sort it ought to be some consolation to know that you haven't got to live forever.

Melville called it the "blackness of darkness."

Clarence Darrow's fiction dealing with the Western Reserve reflects another essence of the lawyer and his art. George Jean Nathan recorded in his notebooks Darrow's assertion that he enjoyed reading aloud to his friends from humorous writers, mentioning specifically among the lawyer's favorites William Dean Howells' farcical drama *The Albany Depot* (1892) — ("She's such a neat, quiet, lady-like person, and all the better for being Irish and a Catholic: Catholics *do* give so much more of a flavor. . . .") — and Don Marquis' satiric *Hermione and Her Little Group of Serious Thinkers* (1916) — ("Don't you think the primitive is just simply too fascinating for anything?"). In his own tales focusing on humorous dramatic incident, Darrow serenely indulged his warm nostalgia for the early days of life and struggle in northeast Ohio and for the people he met as a practicing attorney anxious to make his way in the world. "The Black Sheep," a gentle satire on prodigal children, centers about a theme theological; "The Andover Jail," a farce in slapstick, deals with local politics. Both stories, while showing a marked departure from the dark seriousness of tone that pervades the majority of Darrow's work, nevertheless reflect certain foibles of the human race that are constant and unchanging.

In "The Black Sheep" Daniel Knight, "born and reared in a Calvinistic community in Connecticut," migrated to eastern Ohio and after a time entered a "Unitarian college" which "furnished him a refuge for his doubting mind and troubled soul." Like Amirus Darrow, Knight came to read Voltaire, Paine, Volney, and several other Antichrists, along with the liberal theologians William Ellery Channing and Theodore Parker. Needless to say, Daniel soon is undone spiritually and becomes a shoemaker—a "curiosity . . . to the simple trusting peasants that gathered each Sunday in the big white church that was built upon a hill." His "infidelity did not interfere with his work" and soon Daniel's little shop became a "sort of forum, perhaps not unlike the street-corner in Athens where Zantippe [sic] used to drag Socrates away from his friends and take him home." Farmers and hired men would "crowd" the shop to hear Knight harangue on "the events of the day and the mysteries of life and death." An occasional clergyman would venture into "the dangerous shop" to see if by chance "he might not do something to save this Godless family that seemed wedded to the idols." The shoemaker would not be interested in his "spiritual" soul; he lived only for the *Weekly Tribune* whose editor, Horace Greeley, furnished him ideas on politics, literature, and art. Gradually, the Western Reserve town realized that the Knight children were growing up "in the footsteps of their parents"; all were bright, intellectually-alert—all "loved their books and the studious life." Soon their infidelity, like the father's, came to be taken for granted, and Daniel Knight, feeling proud of his long fight and the strength of devotion to an ideal his life had shown to the townspeople, realized his children "would carry his banner triumphantly" when "he should be forced to lay it down."

One son, however, Ellery Channing Knight, disappointed his father by evincing little concern for books other than those depicting "stories of adventure and wild life on the prairies of the West"; indeed, "It was of Indians and cowboys and stolen maidens that he read." On Sundays when the family would gather to renew their unorthodox spiritual lives together, Ellery Channing, who had bought a gun, "would steal off to the woods and hunt." One day this "wild" young man disappeared and no word concerning his whereabouts was received. Some months later another son, Theodore Parker Knight, returned from a trip to the post office with news. Daniel's reaction to the message concludes the story: "Yes, the letter is from Ellery. He is in Arkansas, a long way off. I was sure something had happened to him. He isn't dead, and I suppose that is something. But he has brought disgrace on me and the family; if the neighbors ever find it out, which I am sure they will, I don't know what I can do. If I had the money I would go down and help him, but of course, I can't. I was always afraid something would happen to him. You all know how hard I tried to raise him right, but I couldn't do it. You remember how he went to Orangeville and was found in a billiard room. You know about his going to Junetown to see a horse race. When he came back I was sure he had been drinking. Anyhow, I smelled something on his breath that I had never smelled before. Then he ran off and went to Maizeville to a camp meeting. He never would work or study. I tried to get him to read the "Age of Reason" but he wouldn't do it. And now, after this, I don't see how I can ever meet the neighbors. To think a child of mine! I don't want to see his face again."

"The mother was crying softly with her eyes fixed on Daniel as he spoke. Finally she said: 'Oh, Father, you are too hard on Ellery. We must stand by him. I never thought he was quite right but he was always good to me. He is my boy and if he ever does come home I will take him back no matter what he has done.'

Theodore could wait no longer.

"Father, father, what has Channing done? Is he in jail? Tell us, what is it?"

"Well, Channing got in with a gang of young fellows down there. I am sure he must have been drinking or he couldn't have done it. They all of them went to a revival meeting, and Channing joined the church. He always was a black sheep!"

"The father and mother opened the door and softly went up-stairs." The humorous suspense and the heavy-handed sentimentalism which bring to a close this domestic "tragedy" characterize the pulp-success formula of O. Henry in the slick literary tintypes of metropolitan dailies. Darrow has taken this journalese treatment and applied it to the enigma of country infidels betrayed by an "erring" son. Shot through with genial satire, "The Black Sheep" affably recounts what might have been in the family of Amirus Darrow had the allurements of orthodoxy entranced a black sheep named Clarence from the irreverent fold.[9]

"The Andover Jail" portrays with broad humor the growing pains suffered by an Ohio village when a young lawyer starts a movement for its incorporation, an ostensible means for effortlessly bringing status and maturity to an otherwise muddy, wooden-sidewalked farm hamlet. Andover during the 1880's, the setting of the story, considered itself "a metropolis"; it boasted a public

[9] The Darrow Papers contain a manuscript copy in the attorney's hand of "The Calf Path" by Sam Walter Foss (1858–1911), Yankee homespun newspaper poet ("The House by the Side of the Road") whose songs "of the average man" were widely syndicated during the late nineteenth and early twentieth centuries. Darrow's preoccupation with earthy expressions of anti-traditionalism is illustrated by his interest in the moralizing of Foss:

> "For men are prone to go it blind
> Along the calf-paths of the mind,
> And work away from sun to sun
> To do what other men have done."

square, two blacksmith shops, a cheese factory, a planing mill, a saloon, an Opera House, two churches, and a public school. A railroad was near by; a canning factory, so rumor told, would soon begin an operation in town. All of "the residents . . . felt sure the place was about to have a boom." Nor was Andover indifferent to the arts. Darrow pointed out that literary societies existed in this Western Reserve town: "Some of the girls had cultivated such a taste for letters that they had read 'Lucille,' " Owen Meredith's "fluent, Byronic, passionate" poem that "thrilled many a fair reader," so Frank Luther Mott tells in *Golden Multitudes*, during the 'eighties when "the cheap publishers sold it by the thousands." Thus, the "boom" for this cultural, as well as economic, mecca was certain to come as soon as "the town put off its swaddling clothes" and incorporated. At election time, the lawyer's crusade for incorporation ended in victory:

> And Deacon Wilhurt, an old-time money changer, promptly announced that he should move outside the city limits a quarter of a mile away where he would not be taxed to death.

The wise deacon foresaw troubled days ahead.

An economic crisis soon develops (salaries for the Mayor, City Solicitor, Board of Aldermen), but the young city struggles with admirable success to meet its initial obligations of maturity, though some townspeople feel that the lawyer—now City Solicitor —had "worked the town to get a job" which he needed to "make up some . . . losses at poker at the county seat." Real complications begin when the town appoints as its marshal, Gib White: "an old soldier and a leading member of the G.A.R. [who] had but one arm and [who] often told of the fierce battle where he lost the missing member," although local citizens actually believed that Gib had lost the arm in a threshing machine. This patriot now gave up a thriving newsstand and peanut wagon to answer his city's call to public service. Marshal White put on a faded uniform and began stalking the avenues in search of burglars and other miscreants. Through Gib's civic clamor, Andover soon is forced to finance street lamps. While salaries for the city administrators continue, the promised boom in real estate does not come. Just when the town is verging on bankruptcy the lawyer makes a startling discovery: "The town had no jail. It was wide open to any attack from the Philistines without." The city had a marshal to arrest desperadoes, a City Solicitor to prosecute them, and a Mayor to sentence them to jail; but, alas, "no prison to put them in." The matter was referred to the town council which, despite the fact that no one had yet been arrested, reluctantly granted the money. After all, "Capital would not come to Andover unless it could feel secure, and how could it feel secure without a jail?"

In one month the jail, "built of wood, and made on the plan of an ice chest" was complete. One year later, there not having been a single occupant, "the town rubbish was accumulating around the box" and local bullies were heard to make irreverent remarks about this landmark. Those who had foolishly led the agitation for a jail seemed destined for local obloquy. Then, "at the darkest hour, Fate seemed to have made up its mind to help their cause." A wealthy fifty-year-old Western Reserve profligate named Chase, desiring to revolt completely against the miserly habits of his late father, began to assemble a traveling circus. In a short time this strange playboy had collected "a horse and wagon, a tent, a monkey, a green parrot, and a bear." He soon found a huge "big darkey" named Bones, who was famous in the area for his feats of strength. This unusual troop headed for Andover, carrying in its wagon "a plentiful supply of firewater." The news of the side-show's imminent arrival set in motion an insidious plan which was subsequently followed. Chase was to be arrested as soon as he became drunk; with no friends to protest, Andoverites hoped that he would pay the fine rather than suffer in prison. He would have occupied the jail; thus, the town would be mollified and the city finances given a substantial transfusion. Shortly after his arrival in Andover, then, the drunken carnival owner was safely asleep in the local jail, with the conscientious Gib White brandishing a pistol over this desperate lawbreaker.

Like the mischievous Dorset boy in O. Henry's famous "The Ransom of Red Chief" who intimidates, brutalizes, and terrorizes the men who kidnapped him, so Chase, with the purest motives of a naive innocence, victimizes the scheming, avaricious conspirators who have brought about his imprisonment. Awakening from his drunken stupor, he asks for food—an item the town legislators have failed to consider providing. White fetches him a meal. In court Chase, to the astonishment and anger of his captors, chooses imprisonment to paying the fine. Furthermore, that evening in the "ice chest" Chase has an attack of the D. T's and the city must finance a doctor, medicines "and other conveniences for the sick":

> [The doctor] told the Marshal he should at once take the patient to the hotel. At this Chase rallied his senses sufficiently to object; he had been sentenced to jail and would stay until his time was out. So Gib went home and got a straw bed and some other comforts for his prisoner and came back.

Round-the-clock nursing care, prescribed by the doctor, was supplied by the Marshal, the City Solicitor, and, finally, the Mayor's hired man. In coherent moments Chase still steadfastly refused to pay his fine. Leaving the door to the "ice chest" open only brought Gib an admonition from his model prisoner, who even refused to leave the jail "for a little exercise." Mrs. White, at length, appeals successfully to the chivalric personality of Chase as she invites him to take a meal with her and her husband. Shortly after the departure of this public enemy

> The Marshall went back to the office to consult with the Mayor and Solicitor. What they said no one ever knew, but a little later a dense cloud of smoke was seen rising back of the Mayor's office. Before many people could reach it, the jail was in flames.

The "big pine box" is soon razed. Gib White returns to his peanut cart; the City Solicitor goes west "to grow up with the country"; the unfortunate Mayor "had so much property in town that he had to stay."

The success of "The Andover Jail," despite Darrow's tendency toward a factual flatness that reduces, somewhat, the comic spirit, lies in his ability to present the gross caricatures who cavort throughout the tale. A major, epical conflict between good and evil involves a weird assortment of villains and a rather unorthodox hero. A new bungling, ineffectual administration created the instrument of its own destruction, and the St. George of Darrow's tale is a fifty-year-old rascal whose intemperance and instability had been the talk of the Western Reserve for years. This farcical episode from the informal history of Andover, with its props and crudities, recounts a collision of fools, a clash of improbables centering about the dramatic endeavor of a town to assert its value. In these terms, one can read "The Andover Jail" as a mock-epic; the regal titans of heroic proportions struggle—against an intoxicated merry-andrew—to maintain the dignity and to balance the budget of their metropolis. Only a Chase recitation of *Lucille* could possibly have added to the tale.

Clarence Darrow often lamented his inability to find enough time for revision and rationalized his literary coarseness by asserting that "his meaning was more important than correctness of wording . . . [that] he wanted . . . his viewpoint [to] reach the public." In one of John Greenleaf Whittier's finest poetic eulogies to a fellow reformer are some lines that might well describe the attorney and his art:

> Yet well I know that thou hast deemed with me
> Life all too earnest, and its time too short
> For dreamy ease and Fancy's graceful sport;
>                               . . . even thy song
> Hath a rude martial tone, a blow in every thought!

Thus, the union of intuition and reality in Darrow's Western Reserve fiction goes beyond the local-colorist literary impulse and transcends the merely comic. The spiritual comedy of Daniel Knight's dilemma at his son Ellery's unexpected, shocking conversion and the comedy of buffoons acted out on the streets of Andover contain insights into a grotesque humanity and stress the complete and utter fallibility of man, his inability to manage Fate and his dire need to submerge intellect and spirit to a hostile or indifferent "correlation of forces" in life. The tale of Ellery Channing Knight and the story of Gib White and company, then, become tragic farces improvised by Darrow out of the raw, black materials of existence. Gib has returned to his peddling of peanuts; Ellery has become respectable. Each cavorts in the little circle of alternatives outlined by Jonathan Edwards in his treatise on Freedom of the Will: man can will to do in the immediate sense, but he can not will to will in the ultimate. Even the humor necessarily encased within this frame becomes charged with irony: "The only thing I ever saw [Darrow once asserted] that to my limited knowledge seemed to have free will was an electric pump I had once on a summer vacation. Every time we wanted it to go, it stopped." Here, then, are justified the limited action and jibes at tradition in the attorney's "sketch book" of life in the Western Reserve, for the emphasis remains on Darrow's contention "that a man has no more to do with his conduct than a wooden Indian," or an erratic electric pump, for "Everybody's life and position are cut out for them." His own enviable career notwithstanding, Clarence Darrow maintained that he was guided by Destiny. Perhaps, like Melville's Captain Ahab, the Chicago attorney was one of the "Fates' Lieutenants."

# Chapter 6

# THE THORNY POINTS

"THE Church and Puritanism rule the thought of the country," Clarence Darrow vigorously asserted during the middle 'twenties; "Intellectually, dogmatism is in the saddle." America, the famed lawyer and fictionist had come to believe, was in the process of complete subversion at the hands of Fundamentalist "blackmailers," and he now devoted much creative energy to the current imbroglio between the Intelligentsia and the Booboisie, between the freethinking disciples of Henry Louis Mencken and an "intellectually disinherited" union of "moral gladiators" whose mores, Darrow felt, bore strong resemblance to the theocratic pattern of existence that had epitomized the uncompromising orthodoxy of the Massachusetts Bay Colony in its palmy days of stewards, stocks, and pillories. The fracas between Anti-Puritan and Neo-Puritan, particularly during the 1920's, assumed proportions of a monumental spiritual dilemma pitting as antagonists the "professional sinhound" who maintained that "moral endeavor" was a full-time profession, and the intellectual "aristocrat" who opposed bitterly the mainstream of Philistinism then pervading the nation in the form of "heresy hunting," censorship, and legislation of morals. The characteristic alignment of Clarence Darrow with the "lunatic fringe" dictated clearly that he support the position of Mencken, "that fake sage of Baltimore," that "noisy, vociferous, and half-baked little man," as the irate Reverend Shannon exploded in a sermon preached to Studs Lonigan and his neighbors; indeed, to support this social menace was to revere an Antichrist whose reading list had been followed, with obvious consequences so the clergyman indicated, by the despicable murderers Leopold and Loeb. Mencken, at any rate, as intellectual doll-baby of all sophisticated thinkers of the day, realized the value of having Clarence Darrow's aggressive, muscular support against "the lubricious Puritan mind" and in the *American Mercury*, a clarion of dissent edited by this "public nuisance," Darrow was identified as "an untiring foe of buncombe in all its forms." In addition, when George Jean Nathan, long a companion of Mencken and another diabolic foe of Neo-Puritanism, devoted fourteen panegyrical pages to Darrow in his "intimate notebooks," at length referring to the attorney as "one of my greatest and deepest admirations," he set down an evaluation shared by all recruits in the Anti-Puritan militia:

> Nearly all the imbecilities he has sought to lay live on. But they are not as safe as they used to be. Someday, let us hope, they will be put down. Whoever at last puts them down will owe half his bays to Clarence Darrow.

Thus the Chicago attorney now directed his pen against tyrannies that fell without the bounds of crime and criminals as defined by the statute books. Eugenics and Prohibition, Fundamentalism and "Boobology" became the targets for his literary fusillades. Darrow's picture in *Vanity Fair* for March, 1927, bore the caption, "A Chicago Lawyer Who Has Become a Militant Figure in the World War on Hypocrisy."

In the name of historical veracity it must be noted that Clarence Darrow maintained a rather circumscribed attitude toward Puritanism, for as a *fin-de-siècle* iconoclast not wishing to see Bohemia invaded he was concerned with the "Blue Law" aspects of this social phenomenon as it manifested itself in American life during the 1920's and 1930's. Everything relating to suffering and self-denial; everything vaguely associated with sin, manners, and morals; everything that intruded between man and his *libido* he unequivocally and enthusiastically labeled as Puritan. Darrow himself might well have written the words of Thomas B. Macaulay, published in 1848: "The Puritans hated bear-baiting, not because it gave pain to the bear, but because it gave pleasure to the spectators." Thus, Puritanism—a force complex in its theological and socio-political ramifications, an intellectual focus whose spiritual consequences had been instrumental in shaping the American mind and character even well into the twentieth century—became reduced to a mere Fundamentalist infringement upon freedom and individualism. Indeed, Prohibition and censorship, two major "Puritan" crusades of the 1920's, were no more related to historical Puritanism than were free-love and burlesque offshoots of New

England Transcendentalism. On the other hand, heresy-hunting, characterized by the Palmer Raids of the early 1920's, when every alien was an incipient "Bolshevik" helping to construct "The Next Soviet Ark," was a peculiar but true manifestation of Neo-Puritanism, directly descended from the very planters of the Bay Colony. In the seventeenth-century cases of heretic Ann Hutchinson and dissenter Roger Williams were revealed the Puritan purge techniques once justified by Nathaniel Ward in *The Simple Cobler of Aggawam* (1645) when he observed that "Novelties of opinions may unravell [sic] the whole texture" of the State, for "The power of all Religion and Ordinances, lies in their purity . . . their simplicity." It is essentially through this tangential relationship, then, that Darrow's viewpoint approached contemporary Puritanism— to the despair of historians, but to the delight of H. L. Mencken and "flaming youth."

During Mencken's tenure as editor of the *American Mercury* eugenists were making a serious bid for national subscription to and, ultimately for adoption of their ideas for improvement of the race. Phrases like "the fruit of the family tree," "tomorrow's children," "being well-born," and "race culture" became part of eloquent rhapsodies emanating from Chatauqua platforms and lecture halls, while Dr. Albert Edward Wiggam—"a sort of cross between Billy Sunday and Einstein"—burst "upon the American public . . . with a happy way of talking science." [10] Wiggam, a eugenic evangelist, exhibited, according to Mencken, "Methodism in a laboratory apron." To both Mencken and Darrow, the cult of Wiggam was another manifestation of Puritanism, and the Baltimore editor's "Eugenic Note" in the *Mercury* of June, 1924, bitterly scathed the advocates of the earnest doctor's thesis that "From dogs to kings, from rats to college presidents, blood always tells." Mencken, in a rather melancholy joke, attributed the Renaissance to the Black Death:

> In less than twenty years it reduced the population of Europe by at least 50%—and yet it left substantially all of the wealth of Europe untouched. More, it killed its millions selectively; the death rate among the upper classes, as every Sunday-school scholar reading the Decameron of Bocaccio knows,

[10] George C. Whitehead (ed.), *Environment vs. Heredity: A Debate between Clarence Darrow and Albert E. Wiggam* (1930), p. 9.

was immensely less than the death-rate among the submerged. The net result was that Europe emerged from the
pandemic with the old pressure of population relieved, all the
worst problems of politics in abeyance, plenty of money, and
a newly-found leisure. The best brains of the time, thus suddenly emancipated, began to function freely and magnifi-
cently.

Not long after this blast at the Wiggamites, Clarence Darrow
joined the troop of *American Mercury* contributors to belabor the
cult of eugenics with more vigor than his famous editor.

In October, 1925, Darrow published an essay on "The Edwardses and the Jukeses," a genealogical analysis concerning "the
surprising adventures of the progeny of one Max Jukes (the villain)
and one Jonathan Edwards (the hero), both pursued by a relentless
fate (the germ plasm)." The author, intent on destroying the
edifice erected by prominent eugenists, stated that evidence in
behalf of this scientific fad "has come from the study of animals
whose love affairs have been controlled and dictated"; he thereupon
began an analysis of individual scions of the famous Edwards
descendants and the notorious Jukes family, assassinating the
hallowed reputation of Jonathan Edwards by labeling the revered
minister as a being whom "Even cold and Puritan New Englanders
could not stand," a divine who "seemed to take joy in the thought of
eternal hell for the wicked," a Calvinist whose religion had a
"ferocious nature":

> This great progenitor of a strong and righteous line, this
> carrier of potent germ-plasm to generate the race, was a lover
> of children . . . [who stated] "As innocent as young chil-
> dren seem to be to us, yet if they are out of Christ they are
> not in God's sight, but are young vipers, and infinitely more
> hateful than vipers. . . .

Darrow catalogued the titles of Edwards's most orthodox hellfire
sermons—"Future Punishment of the Wicked," "Wrath Upon the
Wicked to the Uttermost," "The Misery of Unbelievers," "Of End-
less Punishment"—and quoted the most convulsive portion of "Sinners in the Hands of an Angry God": "The God that holds you over
the pit of hell, much as one holds a spider over the fire, abhors you
and is dreadfully provoked. . . . . . . you are ten thousand

times more abominable in His eyes than the most hateful and venomous serpent is in ours." Thus indicting this preacher as an intellectual menace, "a Fundamentalist, stern and unyielding," Darrow went on to abuse Edwards essentially for the same reasons that later motivated his ruthless cross-examination of William Jennings Bryan at Dayton: the rigorous fundamental reliance on the absolute authority of the Bible as a revealed document. With Jonathan Edwards as a straw man emblemizing for Darrow the embodiment of Puritanism, the extension to present-day moral considerations was readily bridged by the readers. The Puritanism of Edwards, the attorney propounded, fused the theology of John Calvin and the dogmatism of the Mathers with the equally unfortunate "religious affections" of George Whitefield and the Wesleys: predestination and evangelism were the resulting oppressive connotations.

Max Jukes, the "antithesis to Jonathan Edwards," was a hunter, a fisherman, a hard drinker, a person jolly and companionable. While the Edwards line reveals, according to Albert Edward Wiggam, twelve college presidents, 265 college graduates, sixty-five college professors, sixty physicians, 100 clergymen, and the like, the Jukes strain has brought into being sixty habitual thieves, fifty common prostitutes, forty women venereally diseased, and others in similar straits of misfortune. Darrow, however, supported the thesis that mere transmission of germ plasm from Jonathan Edwards was not the sole factor in creating a race of the intellectually and morally elect, but, conversely, the sad tale of the Jukes family "is the story of any number of other families environed as they were." The fate of this clan was inevitable:

> Living in a sterile country, surrounded by poverty, condemned by conditions which have always been common to certain localities, they developed a manner of living and acquired a reputation which as social heritages were passed on from generation to generation. . . . It is the story of the squalid section of every isolated sterile, rural community and of every poverty-stricken city district.

It is, in short, a flagrant begging of the question at hand to compare for eugenic purposes the Jukeses (from a barren, rocky, isolated community) with the Edwardses (from the fertile Con-

necticut valley), for to Darrow the multiplicity of unresolved environmental influences easily outweighs the speculation concerning
suitable or undesirable germ plasm. The entire idea behind such
propaganda in behalf of Eugenics was eventually to create, so
Darrow perceived, a contemporary version of the Elect, an America
of visible, Puritan saints. Such an idea neither Darrow nor Mencken
could tolerate with any charitable feeling. Thus, *Who's Who in
America*, the collection of biographies of "great men" who sired
brave and noble, wealthy and successful progeny, Darrow referred
to as the "human studbook," a term strangely, yet comically,
jarring when employed in a discussion of Jonathan Edwards.

The June, 1926, issue of the *Mercury* published Clarence Darrow's broadside on "The Eugenics Cult," that contemporary American group whose investigations in "degenerate protoplasm" were
making people "shudder with horror at the thought of the rising
tide of undesirables" in their midst. Setting his sights again on the
hosts of nefarious Neo-Puritans whom he saw behind this purgative
social orgy, Darrow pronounced what he felt were the malignant
considerations inherent in the entire eugenics movement:

> The good old *Mayflower* stock is suffering the same unhappy
> fate as the good old pre-Prohibition liquor. It is being mixed
> with all sorts of alien and debilitating substances.

Using an analogy familiar to Bay Colony congregations, Darrow
reiterated the ultimate aim of the eugenics cult: the establishment
of "a simple caste system in which the literate sheep are carefully
separated from the illiterate goats." In a debate with Dr. Lothrop
Stoddard on American immigration policy three years later, Darrow expressed with similar antagonism his passionate hatred for
any restrictive, regulatory influence determined to purify the race;
such impositions, all inspired by contemporary Neo-Puritan trends
in social thought, were aimed at eliminating all minority sentiment
at variance with the Fundamentalism he then observed gripping the
country:

> Are these descendants of the Mayflower such wonderful peo-
> ple? I don't know. They used to hang old women in New
> England for being witches, and everybody knows that an old
> woman couldn't be a witch. These Mayflower descendants are
> the most devoid of human sympathy of any people on the

earth today. What do they care about people? They like to work; that is all.

The eugenics cultist was thus portrayed as a collaborator in an unwholesome crusade to Nordicize and Puritanize the race; his role involved a base profanation of the integrity of mankind and a dangerous tampering with the immutable laws of the universe:

> I am not a blind worshipper of Nature [Darrow wrote]. I can not say whether she is good or bad. Man has no means of knowing. We can say only that, like all life, he is her product, that she is strong, if not invincible, and that she seems to delight in undoing the puny works of those who seek to meddle with her laws.

In the long run, however, the most fearful aspect of the eugenics trend for Darrow was the fact that it was symptomatic of the contemporary plight of America with its facile media for self-culture, self-improvement, and, to borrow the phraseology of the counterpart nineteenth-century paradise-planters, "Perfection." It tended, furthermore, to deify the State or the Committee that would be made responsible for setting up a workable, successful program of selection and sterilization, and for formulating acceptable principles on which to base their human, fallible judgments.[11] Only a warped Fundamentalist, Clarence Darrow firmly believed, could take upon himself with impunity an appointment at the hands of the Almighty as a "steward" and proceed to carry out so anointed a task:

> In an age of meddling, presumption, and gross denial of all the individual feelings and emotions, the world is urged, not only to forcibly control all conduct, but to remake man himself! Amongst the schemes for remolding society this is the most senseless and impudent that has ever been put forward by irresponsible fanatics to plague a long-suffering race.

Indeed, it was "a tough day," Darrow observed, when the Puritans settled in Massachusetts; it will be worse, he indicated, for our

[11] In *Marriage and Morals* (1929) Bertrand Russell noted that an Idaho statute legalized the sterilization of "mental defectives, epileptics, habitual criminals, moral degenerates, and sex perverts." Under this law, suggested the English philosopher, "Idaho would have justified the sterilization of Socrates, Plato, Julius Caesar, and St. Paul."

contemporaries if Neo-Puritans persist in interfering with "the laws of nature." A visionary cult that was regarded skeptically by reputable scientists, as well as lay readers of the *American Mercury*, eugenics was relegated to a more scholarly and less publicized pursuit by World War II in much the same manner as the Civil War effectively terminated the varied schemes of racial perfection born in the enthusiastic minds of transcendentalists and other reformers during another age when things were in the saddle, riding mankind. Darrow, in a sardonic moment, did concede one point to the disciples of Wiggam; he agreed that "men differ": "Some are rich; others are intelligent. Some go to jail; others go to Congress."

While the Anti-Saloon League had been formed in 1893, the completed process of Prohibition was not enacted until 1919, when with the ratification of the Eighteenth Amendment, America sought to undergo the "Noble Experiment"; thus, a treachery was effected by "shrewd shysters" and engineered by "shrewd press agents," according to the smarting, pilsener-drinking H. L. Mencken. Back in 1909 Clarence Darrow had made his first public denunciation of Prohibition in a lecture delivered before the New England United Labor League, in New Bedford, Massachusetts. From this point to Repeal, Darrow entered the battle to curb those forces which were, in moral righteousness, invading the personal liberties of the masses. Not only did he frequently publish articles condemning the Volstead Act and its Puritanical supporters, but he also debated and lectured on Prohibition "in nearly every American city." The Neo-Puritan of the twentieth century had now developed into "a specialist in all forms of public rectitude, from teetotalism to patriotism," and was now a "sacerdotal prop" whose presence on the scene acted as direct inhibitant to creativity. As Darrow bitingly set down in his autobiography, "There would be no literature, no art, no music, no statesmanship if we relied on the prohibitionist for works of genius."

"The Ordeal of Prohibition," Darrow's very first contribution to the *American Mercury*, appeared in August, 1924. Lacking the stump vituperation and forensic excess Darrow often employed in his debates and lectures, the article embodied an intelligent, compelling argument for repeal—a polemic void of sensational cynicism, a highly readable, historical account of certain dubious laws, the people who sponsored them, and the unhappy results of such controversial legislation. Relying very heavily upon the sociology of William Graham Sumner, Darrow, early in the essay, sketched the evolution of all salutary legal acts:

> Most laws grow out of the habits and customs of the people. These customs grow into mores and are finally embodied in laws. Long before statutes are passed, the great mass of men have formed their attitudes and ways of living and the statutes are simply codifications of existing folkways.

In the course of human evolution, however, there have been instances where some "active minority" moved by "religious zeal [or] political intolerance" was able to pass a law that neither originated nor underwent healthful maturative incubation in "the customs and habits of the people." The Catholic and Protestant Inquisitions, prime examples of fanatical legislation and enforcement, began a reign of terror that devastated much of Europe; witchcraft in Salem threatened to devour even the all-Puritan society from top to bottom as secular and non-secular guardians of the law united in a singular purpose whose impulse was based on a hysteria which saw, as another *Mercury* author noted, "a torturable witch in every old woman who had lost her teeth." Such "bad laws" eventually "perished from lack of use" or from repeal; authorities could no longer enforce principles that were repugnant to the majority.

The history of so-called Blue Laws in America, Darrow argued, "furnishes another illustration of the way in which fanaticism burdens the statute-books with oppressive legislation and also of the way in which the common sense of the people finally disposes of it." The lawyer listed historical statutes forbidding travel on Sunday, theater attendance, dancing; he cited laws restricting ladies' hairdos and apparel and quoted from a Puritan regulation passed in November, 1646, which decreed the death penalty "for cursing or striking persons." The builders of the Bay Colony, he noted, went even further:

> Any son which will not obey the voice of his father or the voice of his mother and when they have chastened him will not hearken unto them, then shall his father and mother . . . lay hold on him and bring him to the Massachusetts Assem-

bly in the Court, and if it is proven in Court that their son is
stubborn and rebellious and will not obey their voice and
chastisement, but lives in sundry, notorious crimes, such a
son shall be put to death.

Laws of this nature soon were obsolete. Many similar ordinances
currently "on the books," Darrow stated, are not even worthy of
repeal, for they have long been dead. One pays little heed to the
Sunday laws in many states that forbid "the publication of newspapers, the running of trains and street-cars, riding and driving for
pleasure, attending moving picture shows, [and] playing any
game."

In language derived from Herbert Spencer, then, Darrow related
his journey through some aspects of historical jurisprudence to the
situation at hand: "The force which demands the law is active and
persistent. . . ." The apparent strength of the movement is merely
organization of energy and isolation of the issue. One must maintain "a broad toleration for minorities," the lawyer exclaimed, but

> To enforce the obedience of minorities by criminal statute be-
> cause a mere majority is found to have certain views is tyr-
> anny and must result in endless disorder and suffering.

Without bombast or effusive rhetoric, the author concluded his
essay with brief mention of the more ludicrous effects of Prohibition on the personality of America:

> The acreage of grapes has rapidly increased . . . and the
> price gone up with the demand. The government is afraid to
> interfere with the farmer's cider. The fruit grower is making
> money. The dandelion is now the national flower.

Darrow's conclusion was pungent and brief: Prohibition, its legislation and enforcement, "is both a tragedy and a hoax."

With equal zeal Clarence Darrow debated the Prohibition
question with such luminaries as Dr. Clarence True Wilson,
Secretary of the Methodist Board of Temperance, Prohibition, and
Public Morals; Dr. John Haynes Holmes, popular New York
clergyman; and Wayne B. Wheeler, general counsel for the Anti-
Saloon League of America. In these widely publicized and heavily
attended contests between the Wets and the Drys, Darrow turned
his courtroom technique for potent oratorical suasion on audiences

generally sympathetic to his cause, and Dr. Wilson in a 1931 vaudeville exchange was the recipient of the attorney's most violent excoriation of this "damnedest nonsense ever invented by a set of political cowards":

> He [Wilson] told us where his office is. In Washington. Right close to the House of Congress. In fact, it is the Methodist Vatican. The Methodists have erected the building right close to the House of Congress to bulldoze and browbeat the spineless people that we send to Washington. . . . And then they are worrying the life out of themselves for fear that the Pope of Rome through Al Smith is going to control the country! . . . I have never seen a Prohibitionist in my life who cared how corrupt people were, how dishonest they were . . . if they only kept sober. . . . They will vote for the biggest fools and most corrupt people on earth, if they are dry.

Darrow had, furthermore, come to the conclusion that "the revivalists and temperance lecturers [are] as brothers," as he categorically stipulated in an essay on "Tyranny and the Volstead Act"; and if the inflamed attorney had decided to document the allegation, he could have found much evidence with little trouble, for Billy Sunday's "trail-hitters" were forever ready to take part "in the activities of the Anti-Saloon League." Not only was this a reformist crusade capable of legislating "men out of the slough of despond" but it also became a theo-patriotic force organized and directed against "un-American scapegoats such as unassimilated foreigners, whiskey politicians, saloon-keepers, and booze-soaked labor leaders." These encroachments made by Fundamentalism on politics were early revealed by statements emanating from the Reverend Samuel Porter Jones, noted nineteenth-century evangelist, who observed shortly after the Haymarket Riot of 1886 that

> When you come down to bed-rock, all this communism and Anarchism are based upon the liquor traffic. Where did the Chicago anarchists hold their secret conclaves? In the back part of barrooms.

His definition of Communism was equally simple and colorful:

> It is the 50,000 poor men who have been debauched by whiskey who say they have spent the money which you have been accumulating and they are now calling upon you to divide.

At such sentiments Clarence Darrow leveled his bitterest invectives. He became nearly frenzied when he flayed the "Puritan Protestants" and their constant, traditional opposition "to pleasure." The natural, traditionary home of Prohibition is "in the Protestant churches," he asserted.

> It flourished in the country—in the sparsely settled districts—the habitat of the remaining Puritans in America. It was marked by all the intolerance and bigotry that usually haunt the farms and fastness of American rural life.

The crusade, indeed, Darrow felt was religious in nature. As early as 1919 he had stated from the lecture platform that "The Prohibitionist is not interested in getting rid of rum. He is interested in Prohibition; and when you get rid of rum his job is gone, and he has got to find another." Thus, a portrait of the sincere reformer becomes instead a projection of the blighted fanatic whose quest abjures human values and deteriorates to psychological absurdity.

The Prohibitionist lobbyist was also, Darrow believed, a product of another peculiar aberration of the age; namely, High-Powered Salesmanship, a topic on which he eloquently held forth in the lead article of the *Mercury* for August, 1925. Mencken had billed the essay "How To Be A Salesman" as "A shrewd and humorous lawyer's analysis of the new business necromancy" conjured by a modern advertising which was then revaluating even the life of Christ, discovering in Jesus the progenitor of capitalism. In Bruce Barton's best-seller of 1924–1925, *The Man Nobody Knows: A Discovery of the Real Jesus*, the author offered an opening epigraph "Wist ye not that I must be about my Father's *business?*" [Italics Barton's] and then systematically analyzed Christ as The Executive, The Outdoor Man, The Sociable Man, and The Founder of Modern Business. The power of advertising and salesmanship was best disclosed in Mr. Barton's headline treatment of Christ's career:

PALSIED MAN HEALED
JESUS OF NAZARETH CLAIMS RIGHT TO
FORGIVE SINS
PROMINENT SCRIBES OBJECT
"BLASPHEMOUS," SAYS LEADING CITIZEN
"BUT ANYWAY I CAN WALK," HEALED MAN
RETORTS

To satirize this theological approach to business, Mencken printed an item in the Americana section of the *Mercury:* "The first president of Lion's International was Jesus Christ. I quote you from the Bible: He was 'Lion of the tribe of Judah.'" Darrow by analyzing excerpts from the deluge of salesmanship manuals with their facile and free Bartonesque glibness offered a sharp, probing indictment of the current American mind with its emphasis on boobery, crudeness, and hopeless gullibility. "*Do not permit the Prospect to reason and reflect,*" Darrow quoted in evidence and elaborated on these suggested principles for neophyte salesmen:

> While looking a prospect straight in the eye, *it gives him no chance to reason or reflect.* An idea is planted on the subjective mind. It is not analyzed. It is not compared with some past experience. *It is taken as truth.*

Such ruthlessness of business principle was recognizable as within the Puritan economic ethic, where the so-named Yankee trader for years proudly sported a dubious reputation as sharper and "fast-talker"; for the Almighty recognized the pursuit of material values as a spiritual necessity to ward off frivolous commitments. The worldly acquisitions one made indicated success in this holy dedication. Thus be it also with the Dry, a person with a pseudo-moral product to sell, emphasized Clarence Darrow:

> Nothing that any Prohibitionist does is wrong—it can't be wrong because God tells them it is a good thing and He is going to take care of them when they go to Heaven.

In thus subscribing to the Neo-Puritanism of the 1920's, the proponents of Dryness revealed for the lawyer that they "care nothing about the nature of man, the theories of government, or the lessons of history." When "the grand illusion" was shattered once and for all, Americans quickly "put the memory of Prohibition out of their minds," H. L. Mencken gleefully observed, "just as they . . . put the memory of the great influenza epidemic of 1918–19."

As Darrow's heralded appearance at the Scopes Trial revealed, his concern with popular attempts to theologize secular life in a multiplicity of aspects was pronounced, and he often isolated for special treatment what Max Nordau would have called The Fundamentalist Lie. Along with Mencken the Antichrist, Clarence

Darrow felt that excessive enthusiasm had deteriorated religion until "the rural Baptists, by the route of Fundamentalism, rapidly descended to the dogmas and practices of the Congo jungle." Both iconoclasts argued that "The difference between religions is a difference in their relative content of agnosticism," and Darrow devoted many pages during the latter days of his career to expostulating on "The Absurdities of the Bible," the reasons for his agnosticism, and the "myth of the soul." At times his tone and method were directly in the Mencken tradition, with emphasis mainly on attacking contemporary Puritanical principles in American life. At other times Darrow adopted the historical posture of Lucretius and of certain "Graveyard Poets" in outlining for his readers an atomic theory of civilization and eternity. Antipathy toward what Carl Sandburg called the "contemporary bunk-shooter," the wild-eyed devil-chasing evangelist whose theological common-denominator derived from fearful exploitation of the religious affections and God's tyranny also became a paramount theme in the lawyer's writing which repeated again and again Darrow's belief in science, in determinism, in evolution, and in the conspiracy of Nature's forces—themes on which he had written much fiction in the past.

Henry Goddard Leach, editor of the *Forum*, which published a number of controversial religious articles during the 1920's, wrote in a forward what he regarded the significance of Darrow's essay "The Myth of the Soul":

> Clarence Darrow's discussion of immortality in the present issue is . . . both symptomatic of the times and revolutionary in intent and possibilities. It resolves long scepticism and loose thinking into a positive case . . . It is disturbing—not alone because it challenges old peace of mind, but because its philosophical and practical implications contemplate a new heaven and earth, a new direction for human hopes, and a new doctrine for human labors. If it is true that this life has no sequel, then our codes of conduct and morality, our education, our public and private conscience, our personal liability and responsibility must be reoriented and adjusted to fit the facts.

Written when Darrow was seventy-one years old, this study of belief and immortality attempted to synthesize and to chronicle the spiritual meanderings, flirtations, and investigations conducted during his lifetime by an articulate—at moments, even poetic—foe of orthodox faith. From Paganism to Spiritualism, from the New Testament to Herbert Spencer, Darrow traveled the metaphysical gamut with careful, reflective prose which intimidated the faith of no one, no matter how fundamental his belief in Scripture might be. As the title suggested, Darrow utilized the term "myth" with deliberate ambiguity: both as the collective belief built up over a period of time in response to the wishes of a group, a credo ineffably mystical; and as a traditional tale concerned with deities, demigods, superhumans, usually without a determinable basis of fact or natural explanation.

The Soul, as Darrow treated it, is a legendary force that persists, a "delusion" necessary to soften the harsh duality of body and soul after death when the body disintegrates; "dissolution," Spencer's term became Darrow's term too. The Soul is a flimsy adhesion to spirituality so that the "celestial geography" which sets a heaven above the firmament will be placed within the realm of everyone. Soul does not represent "consciousness"; only through "alchemy" can "resurrection" of so intangible a precept be brought about. The current addicts of Spiritualism—occult reconnoiterers who aroused interest in Hamlin Garland, William Dean Howells, Arthur Conan Doyle, and other literary men—offer "no evidence" to support their extravagant claims to truth. Hysteria and stress, Darrow felt, caused the evident "success" of sorcerers and mediums, along with their seances and trances. At length, Clarence Darrow set forth his positive theory concerning the Soul and immortality. He quoted the "great naturalist" Jean Henri Fabre: "At the banquet of life each is in turn a guest and a dish." The lawyer then continued:

> There is life in all animals and plants and at least potential life in inorganic matter. This potential life is simply unreleased force and matter—the great storehouse from which all forms of life emerge and are constantly replenished.

With this hypothesis, derived "from the modern scientific doctrine of the indestructibility of matter and force," Darrow gave eloquent expression to a philosophy of Paganism subscribing to the realism of a life composed of "Fleeting joys and unavoidable pain" which ultimately bring "a closer kinship" between a humanity of way-farers facing this common destiny. This stance he tempered with his usual measure of Spencerian evolutionism:

> These natural processes of change, which in the human being take the forms of growth, disease, senility, death, and decay, are essentially the same as the processes by which a lump of coal is disintegrated in burning. One may watch the lump of coal burning in the grate until nothing but ashes remains. Part of the coal goes up the chimney in the form of smoke; part of it radiates through the house as heat; the residue lies in the ashes on the hearth. So it is with human life. In all forms of life nature is engaged in combining, breaking down, and recombining her store of energy and matter into new forms. The thing we call "life" is nothing other than a state of equilibrium which endures for a short span of years between the two opposing tendencies of nature—the one that builds up and the one that tears down. In old age, the tearing-down process has already gained the ascendancy, and when death intervenes, the equilibrium is finally upset by the complete stoppage of the building-up process, so that nothing remains but complete disintegration. The energy thus released may be converted into grass or trees or animal life; or it may lie dormant until caught up again in the crucible of nature's laboratory.

The gross heathen denial of life after death, the inevitability of man's utter dissolution according to the laws of Nature, were based on Clarence Darrow's absolute reliance on the logic of science and on the strictures of Paganism. His statements concerning the atomic structure of the universe, the use of "equilibrium" as synonymous with the Doctrine of the Flux, and the mutability of the physical universe place Darrow in exact alignment with Philip Freneau whose "The House of Night" (1779), deriving both from the English "Graveyard Poets" and from the Latin poet Lucretius (*De Rerum Natura*), brought into American letters a macabre type of verse eulogizing Epicurean materialism:

> What is this Death, ye deep-read sophists say?
> Death is no more than one unceasing change;
> New forms arise, while other forms decay,
> Yet all is life throughout creation's range.

> The towering Alps, the haughty Apennine,
> The Andes, wrapt in everlasting snow,
> The Apalachian and the Ararat
> Sooner or later must to ruin go.
>
> Hills sink to plains, and man returns to dust,
> That dust supports a reptile or a flower;
> Each changeful atom by some other nurs'd
> Takes some new form, to perish in an hour.

Clarence Darrow's counterpart in eighteenth-century American Paganism, then, poetized the sentiments the lawyer set forth in "The Myth of the Soul," for the significance of this system holds the core of Darrow's agnosticism and his Voltaire-like desire to free America from what he considered superstition. Since everything undergoes dissolution and decay, the idea of a future life must be renounced; with this rejection comes the realization that no punishment awaits. After death one need not fear divine vengeance or seek divine reward. Death is real when man ceases to exist; only then is he directly concerned with this phenomenon. And in the atomic stockpile of matter the process of Nature ceaselessly works. Darrow, paraphrasing Lucretius, asserted:

> Whatever our faith, we mainly live in the present—in the here and now. Those who hold the view that man is mortal are never troubled by metaphysical problems. At the end of the day's labor we are glad to lose our consciousness in sleep. . . .

The "Myth" of the Soul, to Darrow, then, was a fanciful creation at the hands of zealous theologians, an element of folklore, a theory of infinite symbolic value. He realized that those who subscribe to a belief in ultimate resurrection and immortality derived invaluable spiritual balm. Unable himself to accept these tenets in any form, the attorney put the case this way in a debate on "Does Man Live Again?" (1932):

> Everybody through the ages has been born, and died, and is mixed with all the elements of nature, mixed with snow and wind and sun and heat and cold; until all of us are part of everyone, and every one of us are part of all the rest. . . .
> You are eaten over and over again, and will be as long as life persists.

The Soul? "It is a vague, impossible dream that is born of hope and fear. . . ." Mark Twain noted in his essence of mechanism, *The Mysterious Stranger*, ". . . there is no God, no universe, no human race, no earthly life, no heaven, no hell. It is all a dream —a grotesque and foolish dream. Nothing exists but you. And you are but a thought. . . ." Darrow's dream-soul was a vain spiritual concept incompatible with the materialism his philosophy had exhumed from the Lucretian graveyard.

During the latter years of his life Darrow continued to pronounce publicly that "Bunk suggests religion" and that immortality is merely "a kind of pathetic faith" for senile minds. When he was seventy-two years old, he contributed to the *Saturday Evening Post* an article on what life meant to him at this advanced age, and using a multiplicity of phrases whose journalese connotations tended to surround his case with an authority of power and truth, Darrow continued to stress his favorite nineteenth-century Spencerian concept of the "persistence of force":

> The individual existence is a part of the ongoing power that for a longer or shorter time takes the form and substance of *the special ego.* When for any reason the structure no longer functions, *the life stream* passes into other forms and entities that are able to distribute and utilize the force which the old organism could no longer house. [Life] soon sinks back into the great *reservoir of force*, where memory and individual consciousness are at an end. [Italics mine]

"I feel with Herbert Spencer," Darrow wrote in attempting to explain his agnosticism, "that whether the universe had an origin— and if it had—what the origin is will never be known by man." And while he consented, because he needed money, to tour the country deliberately pleading causes so unpopular with the masses, Darrow realized that his career illustrated for many what Voltaire's achievements had symbolized for Timothy Dwight, "the triumph of infidelity"; in fact, Darrow noted in his own essay on Voltaire that

> No iconoclast can possibly escape the severest criticism. If he is poor he is against existing things because he cannot succeed. If he is rich, he is not faithful to his ideals. The world always demands of a prophet a double standard. He must live

a life consistent with his dreams, and at the same time must obey the conventions of the world. He cannot be judged either by one or the other, but must be judged by both. In trying to live up to both standards, one invariably misses both. It is hard to be true to the two, especially when the standards of the new and the old are in conflict. The ravens should feed the iconoclasts, but they don't.

The superstition hunt of Paine and Voltaire was the intellectual prototype that urged Clarence Darrow to publicize the cult of agnosticism along with the truisms of Menckenism. Frequently he alluded to the ignominious stain of witchcraft—the "vulgar" sorcery that for Darrow and his coterie narrowly exemplified Puritanism and all of its "blue law" restrictions. Often he referred to "sacred charms" and "revealed religion"—embodying for Darrow the pernicious cloud of Fundamentalism then infiltrating the American character and invading the most private and sacred intellectual and spiritual considerations of man. As in the days of theocracy the individual who defected in religious thought was believed to be morally perverted. To advance the repellant, anti-Christian theories that fell so glibly from the lips of the criminal lawyer and that appeared in widely read organs of popular communication was to seek public abuse and a kind of Pagan martyrdom. Yet Darrow himself pleaded for universal toleration as eloquently as did Roger Williams, who fell from grace in the Bay Colony.

In the manuscript of "A Trip to Holy Land," Clarence Darrow recorded a pilgrimage for the purpose of investigating Old World culture and comparing its values with the New. He based his analogies on an idea Mencken had expressed in 1926:

> Try to imagine a French Wayne B. Wheeler, or a Spanish Billy Sunday, or a German William Jennings Bryan. It is as impossible as imagining a Coolidge in the Rome of Julius.

Darrow, having spent three weeks in Europe, Asia, and Africa composed some twenty pages of recollections and reflections prompted by this grand tour; and while some of the tourist commentary is strongly reminiscent of Mark Twain and other rock-ribbed patriots first exposed to the culture of the ancient world, Darrow's judgments had timely relevance to our own country, its current intellectual status and heritage and its contemporary concern with morals and religion. Naples impressed the lawyer for the beauty which "Nature" had bestowed, but "The old city of Rome is not very interesting":

> Like most things in life, the pictures are better than the real thing. The Forum is not as much of a forum as the Garrick Theater in Chicago. . . . I took no superstition with me; I brought none back; I haven't been converted.

In Egypt, however, Darrow encountered a type of Christian missionary work that once drew the wrath of Herman Melville who had written in *Omoo* of a "Taboo Day" which proclaimed "the sanctity of the Christian Sabbath" and which encouraged the "strict moralities of Christianity" to clash fiercely with the innate softness of the islanders. Darrow noted:

> One realizes that there are people who are civilized; that there are people of intelligence and force, who probably will persist after our civilization is cold, who are not Christians; that there are religious people who believe what they profess; that there are Mohammedans who set up their idol of one God as against what they consider the idolatrous religion. . . . We can teach them nothing. We have made some progress in Christianizing them.

The American observer passed some remarks on the Pyramids, "great monuments of stone" based on a religious deception and serving "as graves for kings"; thus, a "political superstition" as well. If the "halo, the mysticism or the legend" were to be stripped from these archaeological wonders, "a monument twice as high would be twice as interesting." Scoring all types of orthodoxy, Darrow set down another phenomenon these travels brought to his attention:

> I never could understand the mystery of [Egyptian] female apparel. . . . But anyhow, I found out. It was a chapter of the Koran they carried with them so that if they got run over by a jackass or a Ford they could read the Koran while they were dying. All the religious women of India carry it, I am told.

These occasional peculiarities, however, were in no way comparable to the current fixations deluding Americans, who still maintain a smug, chauvinistic superiority toward foreigners:

Years ago I read a "fool" book [Darrow stated] which has been translated into every language of every land and praised by all the hundred per cent Americans and preachers in the world called "The Man Without a Country." It has been used as literature in the schools, pointed out as a model story written by a New England Preacher, Edward Everett Hale.

What the wandering Phillip Nolan wanted was "not a country," Darrow affirmed, "but a place where he could land. He wanted a land place." Anyone who has ever taken a sea voyage, the lawyer suggested, knows the feeling. Darrow concluded his journal with this axiom:

They [foreigners] understand more about the joy of living. We, Puritans, over here, think it is wicked to have fun and anything that adds joy to life is a sin.

Thus, the physical and intellectual peregrinations of Clarence Darrow invariably returned to his pet anathema of the day: Neo-Puritanism and its crusade to cleanse the manners, morals, and religious principles of a nation. The demoralizing tedium of existing day by day under so strenuous a regime was unknown to the wanderer without a country, whose dream of America differed from the reality of life there in the twentieth century. Mencken had pointed out that "the American Puritan was made for satirists as catnip was made for cats," and unsubtle as Darrow's ridicule was, his intent was not to demolish America and its prevailing institutions. Rather, stung by a succession of emotional, evangelical orgies that aroused the moral indignation of many people, he saw a dangerous trend at its inception: the submersion of the intellectual and the immersion of the self at the hands of Fundamentalism; he perceived the serious implications of so-called "togetherness" and "belonging" as well as the logical ostracism of the iconoclast and "freethinker."

The Reverend John Haynes Holmes stated that in Clarence Darrow's "own life he demonstrated the reality of the religion which he denied"; the years spent as defender of lost causes and the numerous humanitarian crusades this attorney for the damned undertook can be called to witness the pastor's evaluation. As did his friend Mencken, Darrow served a particular function in America of the 'twenties and 'thirties; namely, he represented a

segment of the national conscience; a skeptic able to handle himself as a mature controversialist; an articulate spokesman fearless
before the harassments of superimposed, organized morality and
the bludgeonings of intellectual and spiritual bullies; a person
whose only fear was for a groping populace being led, so he dis-
cerned, by mountebanks and charlatans, living in the type of
hapless gaiety and carnivalism emblemized by Dayton, Tennessee,
in August, 1925. A theological Pagan, a philosophical materialist
("Herbert Spencer in his 'First Principles' has shown how impossible it is to find the ultimate explanation," Darrow recorded.
"The theologian, the evolutionist, and the one who views life as
I do, must sooner or later say, 'I do not know.'") A literary
naturalist, Clarence Darrow, in an age increasing its demands for
conformity of belief and action, tried in his writings to cry out
against the Comstock revival of his day, to warn against further
encroachments on individual liberty and intellectual and moral
privacy. From the present-day perspective one can readily see that
what began as heresy-hunting in theology widened to include investigations of social deviation, finally encompassed political de-
fection and, at length, guilt by association. The Fundamentalist
crusade, Darrow would say, marched on.

Darrow maintained consistently the philosophical viewpoint on
which he had settled in the nineteenth century and which he
propagated with force throughout his career in courtroom, in
lecture hall, and by his words on the printed page. "The Skeleton
in the Closet," one of the essays in *A Persian Pearl* (1899), comprised a study in which the then rising Chicago attorney gave expression to his theory of naturalistic immortality:

> Life is a never-ending school, and the really important lessons
> all tend to teach man his proper relation to the environment
> where he must live. With wild ambitions and desires un-
> tamed, we are spawned out into a shoreless sea of moving
> molecules of life, each separate atom journeying on an un-
> known course, regardless of the countless other lives it meets
> as it blindly rushes on; no lights nor headlands stand to point
> the proper way the voyager should take, [sic] he is left to sail
> an untried bar across an angry sea.

The "universal power," however, at this point in the development
of Darrow's thought was an "infinite, *loving* presence" [italics

mine] which eventually "will ever claim us as a portion of its self until our smallest fragments return once more to earth, and are united with the elements from which we came." This "loving" force, transcendentalist in its spiritually progressive implications, metamorphosed considerably through the years as the youthful idealism of Darrow went off, as Hamlin Garland recorded, "into a dark and tangled forest land." By 1925, the force ferrying man on his journey was "Nature, red with tooth and claw," not the Nature of "myths and lullaby tales." Darrow had clearly forsaken the ethic of Emerson for the views of Lucretius and Spencer. In the 'twenties he had come to note:

> Nature is not necessarily good or bad. She is simply all-powerful. She brings some happiness to many; she likewise brings misery to all. . . . No one can point at Nature, blind, cruel, unpitying and say there is anything good in Her. Perhaps there is nothing bad in Her, but certainly nothing beneficent. And, as to man, he is helpless in her hands. In her blindness, she has developed him as he is. Just as she has developed everything else as it is. His limitations are fixed.

To the correspondent struggling for life in Stephen Crane's classic of naturalism "The Open Boat," Nature "did not seem cruel . . . nor beneficent, nor treacherous, nor wise. But she was indifferent, flatly indifferent." For McTeague, Frank Norris's Nietzschean dentist pursued to Death Valley wastes, "The great mountains of Placer County had been merely indifferent to man; but this awful sink of alkali was openly and unreservedly iniquitous and malignant." Darrow's fictional artistry had also examined and sustained these hostile theories; yet, bucking the inevitable odds (supermen like Norris's McTeague and London's Wolf Larsen were eventually reduced to impotence) the lawyer sought to aid this helpless being even as Nature snapped the whip. The step from literary naturalism to social iconoclasm was slight; the so-called "pianissimo revolt" of the 'nineties with its animus aimed at tradition and respectability drew subscribers like Stephen Crane and Harold Frederic from the hosts of Naturalists, and when Clarence Darrow diverted his major literary consideration to an examination of America's social blight, his value as a "debunker" was quickly recognized. In the 'twenties and 'thirties when "Repression became the American illness," Clarence Darrow's voice strongly echoed, "Repression and death go together." He was, in short, a leader in the new army of the antibourgeoisie and with the courage America had long since come to expect of him, wrote and railed against the current fad for vigilantes in our midst, all the time feeling that the human race was in a marked state of spiritual degradation. As the attorney informed an audience which had come to hear him debate Professor Frederick Starr: "We haven't got beyond Plato, and Aristotle and Socrates, although we have Mary Baker Eddy and Dowie and Billy Sunday and Bryan!" On another occasion Darrow enumerated the multitude of elixirs that have afflicted society in the past and that now ineradicably defile our contemporary social reformers and philosophers: "We have had Karl Marx and Henry George, and Billy Sunday and Billy Bryan, and Lydia Pinkham. . . . We have had Christian Science and Free Silver; we have had Peruna [and] Cod Liver Oil. . . ."

Darrow with skill and vision needled the fallacies of modern America, often directly blasting the consecrated army of demagogues whose Puritanism was bringing intellectual and spiritual sterility to the country, a nation now characterized by the angry attorney as

> A mad-house where the human mind is paralyzed and the human lips are dumb for fear of the money changer! We have destroyed . . . the free institutions that it took centuries to rear; we have made a psychology that causes us to look back at Herod and the Duke of Alva and the Witchburners and admit that they were pikers compared with us!

Liberalism and tolerance had fled the American scene, and none but an old-guard reform-Darwinian would be calculated to feel the loss so heavily. George G. Whitehead, who managed a Darrow tour of the lecture circuit, referred to the lawyer, paradoxically, as an "Evangelist"; one, however, who endeavored to purvey to the masses "sane thinking" rather than a combination of God, Kultur, and the Wild Eagle.

Behind all of Darrow's onslaughts against the old Puritanism and the new lay a monumental paradox: he was repelled by Puritans, but his literary sensitivity was attracted to many a device that had characterized discourses cascading from Bay Colony pulpits of the seventeenth century. Utilizing "the plain style," that invocation coming "*out of the wildernesse,*" hell-fire preachers had expostulated upon God's Providences and man's weakness in sermons "mechanically and rigidly divided into sections and subheads . . . [appearing] on the printed page more like a lawyer's brief than a work of art." [12] In his courtroom summations it became Darrow's talent to fuse this "brief" with another dimension and thus to achieve a literary conflict that elevated his pleas into the realm of art. The tension was generated from the presence of two genuinely Puritan traits tugging at his intellect: the Puritan concept of style, which he admired; and the Puritan concept of Liberty, (". . . liberty is subjection to authority . . . ," stated John Winthrop) which he abhorred. Clarence Darrow's "plain style," therefore, was directed to challenge any authority that was not tempered with humanitarianism and compassion, and each client became a universal symbol whereby not the individual but rather a series of moral and ethical considerations was paraded before a tribunal.

One can cite this technique in Darrow's work as early as 1898 when he told a jury:

> Here is Thomas I. Kidd. It is a matter of the smallest consequence to him or to me what you do; and I say it as sincerely as I ever spoke a word. No man ever entered the struggle for human liberty without measuring the cost. . . . But, gentlemen, I do not appeal for him. That cause is too narrow for me, much as I love him and long as I have worked by his side. I appeal to you, gentlemen, not for Thomas I. Kidd, but I appeal to you for the long line—the long, long line reaching back through the ages, and forward to the years to come— the long line of despoiled and downtrodden people of the earth.

When in 1912 Darrow defended himself against a charge of jury bribing he transmuted his case into a universal complex:

> There may be and doubtless are many people who think I did seek to bribe . . . but I am not on trial for that. . . . I am on trial because I have been a lover of the poor, a friend of

[12] Perry Miller, *The New England Mind: The Seventeenth Century* (Cambridge, 1954), p. 332.

the oppressed, because I have stood by labor for all these years, and have brought down upon my head the wrath of the criminal interests in this country.

At the trial of twenty Communists in 1920, men "arrested and charged with advocating the overthrow of the government by force," Darrow categorically stated to the jury:

If you want to convict these twenty men, then do it. I ask no consideration on behalf of any one of them. . . . They are no better than any other twenty men; they are no better than the millions and tens of millions down through the ages who have been prosecuted—yes, and convicted in cases like this. . . . I am interested in the verdict of this jury as to whether this country shall be ruled by the conscienceless men who would stifle freedom of speech when it interferes with their gold; or whether this jury will stand by the principles of the fathers and, whether so far as you can, you will stop this mad wave that threatens to engulf the liberty of the American citizens.

In behalf of Leopold and Loeb, Darrow affirmed

You may hang these boys; you may hang them by the neck until they are dead. . . . I am pleading for the future; I am pleading for a time when hatred and cruelty will not control the hearts of men. . . .

Thus the spokesman was no longer a lawyer of the here and now endeavoring to circumvent statute. He became by the newly revealed grandeur of his cause an interpreter of what Spencer had called Social Statics—an artist intent on revealing and preserving the basic integrity of the human personality. With the homely, effective rhetoric of a Thomas Hooker, Darrow presented the anti-Puritan sentiments of a Thomas Brattle who, in meditating on the Salem Witchcraft Trials, had observed: "I never thought Judges infallible; but reckoned that they, as well as private men, might err. . . ." The jury in the Kidd Case brought in a "Not Guilty" verdict after deliberating less than an hour. At his own trial Darrow was acquitted in thirty-four minutes. While the twenty Communists were found "Guilty," sixteen of them were pardoned before they had served a day of their sentences. In perhaps his most dramatic case, Darrow saved the "compulsion" killers from the death penalty, and although Richard Loeb died in prison, Nathan Leopold, expressing a sincere "desire to devote the rest of [his] life to others as a further expiation for [his] crime," was paroled after serving thirty-two years in Joliet prison. Now, a rehabilitated individual, he can stand as symbolic justification for the plea that spared his life. Darrow's courtroom artistry in its fusion of literary insight and sympathetic judgment was, clearly, imaginative, sound, and effective.

Edgar Lee Masters in 1922 composed a moving eulogy to the combined legal and artistic attributes that made up the creative intelligence and vibrant sensitivity of Clarence Darrow, his sympathy for all those martyred by the world. With this sympathy implicit in his ethic, Darrow took the basic plan of the Puritan sermon, fashioned it with his facility for purveying human drama, tempered it with a singular poetic humanitarianism, and filled it with a sense of the timely, the contemporaneous whose image was necessarily simple, direct, and complete. While he had etched in his mind the exciting vision of Colonel Bob Ingersoll and while he carried under his arm the collected precepts of John Peter Altgeld, Clarence Darrow doubtlessly felt the influential shadowings of seventeenth-century Bay Colony divines peering ominously over his shoulder as he lumbered toward the jury box. Indeed, in his writings as well as his summations, the force of Puritanism in legitimate and illegitimate forms exerted a depth of influence even beyond the realization of the attorney himself.

# Epilogue

## "I Have Always Felt Sympathy . . ."

A LETTER written February 23, 1932, by Brand Whitlock
gave Albert Bigelow Paine notice of a forthcoming book:

> I haven't seen Darrow's Autobiography; he was at work on it
> when he was here [Cannes], and he wrote me not so very long
> ago that it was done. He said a funny thing in his letter; he
> said that everybody was writing his autobiography nowadays;
> that everybody was standing on the street corner beating a
> bass drum and crying: "For God's sake, look at me for a
> minute!"

Despite his denigrating jibe at the autobiographers, Darrow's
own life story was about to appear and in 1932, when *The Good
Earth* was leading the best-seller lists for the second consecutive
year, the attorney published his most popular volume, *The Story
of My Life*, a work which encompassed a backward glance over
the most arresting high spots of his public career. In this volume
that climbed to number nine on the yearly non-fiction popularity
poll, Darrow said nothing at all about his literary ambitions or desires; yet the Muse beckoned consistently and strongly even in
the lawyer's later years. "He felt too old now [1928] to tackle the
long novel he had been contemplating for twenty years; instead he
started work on his autobiography. . . . He was to call the book
*The Story of My Life*, though it might more accurately have been
called *The Story of My Philosophy*. . . ." Indeed, Darrow's song
of himself, almost a soft-spoken monologue with overtones of
*apologia*, scattershoots through his years in Kinsman and Chicago, his association with Altgeld and Debs, his attractions to
Anarchy and Evolution, and his excoriations of Prohibition and
Capital Punishment. Cases and epochs were mirrored; interludes
snatched from the past were underwritten with an attraction as
compelling as a series of newspaper headlines from "only yesterday." M. L. Ernst, a sympathetic reviewer, noted in *Books* (February 7, 1932):

In between all of the philosophizing about the outrages of
penal institutions, the trickery of the law or his [Darrow's]
valuation of living we find few glimpses of the main springs
of this soft giant. The thousands who have followed his career with joy will be astounded that such simplicity could
attain so much success. The many others who believe him to
be the ogre of our times will be disappointed at the absence
. . . of any hate or envy or bitterness.

Other critics praised the style of Darrow's ". . . simple and often-
moving prose"; they observed his philosophy as being "derived
from Tolstoy but shrewdly shaped by the witty and stoic outlook
of a democratic Midwest." However, the facility with which he
declared his lack of elixirs, nostrums, and panaceas for an age
evidently suffering from Fundamentalist fever and the fervent
sincerity with which he constantly asserted his belief in humanity,
despite its biological shortcomings and spiritual misdirections,
radiated from a man governed by impulses (mostly beneficent) and
attitudes (mostly humanitarian). In the Yale *Law Journal* appeared
a statement which stands also as a defense for the seemingly non-
esoteric constituents so inherently a part of Clarence Darrow's
thought:

His book is a combination of an absorbing narrative with
philosophical excursions into the nature of crime, the nature
of the human mind, and the nature of life itself. The sophisticated may criticize the philosophy as naive, the psychiatry as
sentimental, and the theories of crime as emotional. As abstract ideas they lack critical analysis. But in their defense it
should be said that Darrow is not attempting to add to the
sum total of human knowledge but rather to increase human
tolerance.

One cannot question the candor and the sincerity of the matter-of-
fact way in which Darrow summarized the motivating forces behind his highly publicized escapades:

If I have been charitable in my judgments of my fellow man;
if I have tried to help him as best I could; if I have done my
utmost to truly understand him, I know why I have taken this
course—I could not help it. I could have had no comfort or
peace of mind if I had acted any other way. I have been interested in the study of man, and the motives that move and

control his life. . . . I have followed my instincts and feelings and sought to rescue the suffering when I could. But I
know that I have done it more or less involuntarily as a part
of my being, without choice, and without stopping to weigh
which were most deserving or worth saving. If I had paused,
I should probably still be wondering and doing nothing. I
claim no credit, and I want no praise.

The man of affairs was subservient to the call of suffering which
brought Darrow in direct contact with the "clay for his model-
ing": the despoiled of society. Darrow, whose now legendary anti-
clericalism had earned him a high place among American Antichrists, maintained an agnosticism, which was, contradictory to
say, Christian in motivation—a type of cultural theology dependent
wholly and completely on a system of ethics and morals, deistic in
concept and derived from the chaotic and contrastive Design,
rather than from the Biblical revelation, of the universe.

*The Story of My Life* gave expression both by direction and in-
direction to this complex theological pattern, which, to Darrow,
completely humanized religion. In the forty-seven chapters of his
autobiography the ethic and the aesthetic of the attorney were
unified by the ever-underlying principle of human dignity and
honor. Ranging through the turbulent years of his life, the author
capsuled some moods and reveries that formlessly brushed by his
mind at the moment. He rambles as if he and his reader were sitting around the cracker barrel, but Darrow writes, nevertheless,
with a deliberately unpolished urbanity, deceptive with its seem-
ing lack of sophistication. Homely, naive, and hopelessly romantic
is, ultimately, the intellectual and spiritual codification Clarence
Darrow made of Nature and its laws; utilitarian in the extreme,
his beliefs still enabled him to practice those virtues of toleration,
self-reliance, independence, and charity which the social schema
of any age regards as most desirable and good.

A man whose native pessimism was motivated by an innate
idealism, Darrow's quarrel with the universe and his adjustment to
its terms were given harmonious expression at the conclusion of
his chapter on "Delusion of Design and Purpose":

The strongest in intellect and prowess live the longest. Nature, in all her manifestations, is at war with life, and sooner
or later will doubtless have her way. No one can give a reason

for any or all of the manifestations which we call life. We are like a body of shipwrecked sailors clutching to a raft and desperately engaged in holding on. Men have built faith from hopes. They have struggled and fought in despair. They have frantically clung to life because of the will to live. The best that we can do is to be kindly and helpful toward our friends and fellow passengers who are clinging to the same speck of dirt while we are drifting side by side to our common doom.

With the grizzled consistency and tenacity of a grasping "microbe" fighting to survive on this smallest bit "of matter that floats in the great shoreless sea of space" Clarence Darrow maintained the views of evolution and dissolution throughout his life, re-working their metaphorical significance and literary analogies to solve the dilemmas which the Muse occasionally presented. He had discovered this formula early, and it runs throughout the canon of his thought and art like a steel cable, constantly kept in repair and polished to a glitter every day. Spencer and Darwin, along with their philosophic and literary satellites, sufficed Darrow's need for a workable *modus vivendi;* the innate drama of evolutionism, its barren presentation of the socio-economic issues of the day, and its collision with the theological Fundamentalism of Genesis were dynamos which generated the art of this unusual lawyer.

Early in 1931 Clarence Darrow, now hitting the debate circuit on forays that took him at the age of seventy-one from New York to Omaha and from Philadelphia to Tampa, opposed on the lecture platform G. K. Chesterton; the topic, "Will the World Return to Religion?" Public debate, the type of semi-intellectual vaudeville which a paying audience supported, presented an atmosphere, at best, defiantly opposed to the spirit of scholarship and truth; at worst, a popularity contest in which the spirit of evil was to be soundly trounced by the force of good. Originality and subtlety were always forsaken in open debate; niceties of language, creativeness of expression were sacrificed for superficiality and glibness. Issues and results were carefully selected with a conciliatory precision, although it was always fair game to blister Prohibition as freely as the audience would allow. Darrow, forced by financial setbacks to indulge in this now obsolete form of public entertainment, emerged from the circuit with a somewhat damaged reputation. Admirers began to perceive a shallowness in his liberalism and to feel that their idol did not embody all those traits of Modernism which he himself had found utterly lacking in William Jennings Bryan. A brief review from the *Nation*, a magazine sympathetic to Darrow, reveals a sad assessment of his "late" career:

> Mr. Chesterton's argument was like Mr. Chesterton, amiable, courteous, jolly; it was always clever, it was full of nice turns of expression, and altogether a very adroit exhibition by one of the world's ablest intellectual fencing masters and one of its most charming gentlemen. Mr. Darrow's personality, by contrast, seemed rather colorless, and certainly very dour. His attitude seemed almost surly; he slurred his words; the rise and fall of his voice was sometimes heavily melodramatic, and his argument was conducted on an amazingly low intellectual level. Ostensibly the defender of science against Mr. Chesterton, he obviously knew much less science than Mr. Chesterton did; when he essayed to answer his opponent on the views of Eddington and Jeans, it was patent that he had not the remotest conception of what the new physics was all about. His victory over Mr. Bryan at Dayton had been too cheap and easy; he remembered it not wisely but too well. His arguments are still the arguments of village atheists of the Ingersoll period; at Mecca Temple he still seemed to be trying to shock and convince yokels.

One would find it difficult to refute the reviewer's concluding comment, for in many of Darrow's debates, particularly the ones centering about religion, the lawyer maintained a crossroads agnosticism with the same vehemence Colonel "Bob" Ingersoll had formerly displayed while flaying middlewestern horseback preachers of the past. In his writings and in his summations, Darrow never approached the level on which many of his debates were painfully set:

> And the soul. Now, just imagine all the preachers who are talking this fool nonsense. Did they ever tell you where the soul is; where it goes to; how it fools away its time—except to go and sit on a cloud and play a harp? Gracious, I should like that job for 100 million years.

Idea and method became artless and trite:

> Now, I have proved to you that nobody believes in a future
> life, because if a man will travel all over the world, and get
> cut to pieces by inches, in pain all the time, and know that
> death is certain just so he can tack a few more hours onto his
> earthly existence, what is the answer to that?

During a 1931 debate on "Is Religion Necessary?" the ageing attorney reduced even this benighted topic to absurdity:

> Suppose a doctor comes and tells you that something is ter-
> ribly wrong with you and you had better make your will, be-
> cause within one week you are going to Goofville; you were
> not going to take your body with you, but you were going;
> leave your body here and start off to Goofville. You are not
> going for a year but you are going for all eternity. Millions
> and millions and trillions of eons in Goofville. Don't you sup-
> pose you would try to find out where Goofville was and where
> you were going and how you were going . . . ? . . . by
> airplane or submarine or ship or railroad . . . ?

Truthfully, this is the hayseed intellectual pontificating for his
spellbound associates in the general store. Bryan, perhaps, as the
critic suggested, had been too easy. Darrow did not possess the
equipment to enter the realm of Biblical controversy and disputa-
tion inhabited by reputable theologians; rather, to strike at the
most apparent fallacies of Fundamentalists and hyper-zealous re-
ligionists from the music hall stage was to be his unworthy lot
during the last years of his career. He was admired by Emanuel
Haldeman-Julius—the publisher of the "Little Blue Books," professional iconoclast and free-thinker—who saw in Darrow "the
bearing of a philosopher." Most frequently, however, the attorney
in old age was a tradition being commercialized by booking agents
and impresarios. Nevertheless, the reputation which excellence in
the law courts had deservedly brought to him remained cherished
and inviolate—an American legend in jurisprudence.

If Darrow toward the close of his life seemed to be catering to
the so-called middle-class intellects, it was, perhaps, because the
inconstancy of time had wrought some drastic changes on the aggregate personality of America. More sophisticated minds had by

this age picked up the cudgels he had ceased to wield as a professional humanitarian. More talented authors were giving expression to his ethical views and aesthetic responsibilities. His novels with their blundering crudeness and chaotic power became literary curios having attraction only for the historian. The causes that made up the central body of material from which the artist drew were passing as the "home builders" of Frederick Jackson Turner had passed from the frontier. Yet, when the full impact of Darrow's personality is regarded totally, with no attempt to distinguish any singular area of achievement, it is easy to see the mythical stature of the man: the blurred vision becomes one of a crusader, an artist, a humanitarian. Doubtlessly, Clarence Darrow was an intellectual gadfly who, like dissenters in the Massachusetts Bay Colony, would calculatedly disturb the peaceful flow of business conducted by the allegedly respectable. He was, too, a moral firebrand in the very best tradition of American "paradise planters," during our own times in pursuit of the nineteenth century abstract ideal of Perfection. He was an American author, whose undisciplined non-academic literary productions evince more quality than the indiscretions of a conspicuous dilettante. Part Freudian, part Muckraker; cynic and skeptic; romantic and idealist, Darrow brought to the concept of the American dream the disturbing realities unearthed by researches of the nineteenth-century scientists and applied to the American conscience a shrewd cynicism that looked beyond the mere "sour note" in our humor of the post-Civil War period. With a machete poised over any vestige of what he considered Puritanism, albeit by his own limited concept of this cultural force, and a spirit intermingled with middlewestern soil, Darrow gave support to American realism during the days of Comstockery and tenacity to American academic freedom during the days of Bryanism. Fusing the regional and the universal, juxtaposing Relative intangibles of good and evil in insoluble Absolute conflicts, and propagandizing for social progress, Darrow is revealed as a son of the nineteenth century, reared in idioms of Evolution and Perfection. He carried these unshakable principles into the new century and became so vital an emblem of Modernism that he stalks Main Street even today and haunts academic communities as a living myth of courage and freedom of thought.

Grotesque, perhaps, but this lawyer who waged "a thousand

battles," who "had been through more wars than a whole regiment of Pershings" and who participated "in struggles to the death, without codes or quarter" bears analogy to Childe Harold, the "vagrant Childe" of Byron, "inly sad" on a nebulous pilgrimage during which he becomes part of all those he encounters on this transcendental migration. Darrow's journey among the barbarians of the universe encompassed the stammering years of America's young adulthood. His presence along the way added much to the tumultuous years into which the lawyer was, as he liked to think, haphazardly thrown. In spite of his feeling that reality is grim, that futility and dread of annihilation are requisites for straight thinking, and that poverty and relentless fate haunt mankind constantly, the infinite paradox on which he built all of his work and art predicated the hope "that tomorrow will be less irksome than today." Clarence Darrow penned his own epitaph: "I have always felt sympathy for all living things, and have done the best I could to make easier the lot of those wayfarers whom I have met on my journey through the world."

# BIBLIOGRAPHICAL NOTE

Along with those sources cited in the text, these works have been
essential to the study of Clarence Darrow as a man of letters,
his thought and his times:

Aaron, Daniel. *Men of Good Hope: A Study of American Progres-
sives* (New York, 1951). Seminal study of "Precursors" and
"Prophetic Agitators" whose ideas gave direction to social and
literary reformism.

Altgeld, John Peter. *Live Questions* (Chicago, 1899). A compen-
dium of the governor's "papers, speeches and interviews; also
his messages. . . ."

Asbury, Herbert. *Gem of the Prairie: An Informal History of the
Chicago Underworld* (New York, 1940).

Barnard, Harry. *"Eagle Forgotten": The Life of John Peter Altgeld* (New York, 1938). A standard work.

Boyd, Ernest A. *Portraits: Real and Imaginary* (New York, 1924).
Unsympathetic attitude toward Puritanism by a popular commentator of the 1920's.

Cargill, Oscar. *Intellectual America: Ideas on the March* (New
York, 1941). A sound, incisive evaluation of Darrow as a
writer along with an exhaustive study of the "ideodynamics"
molding American civilization.

Commager, Henry Steele. *The American Mind: An Interpretation
of American Thought and Character Since the 1880's* (New
Haven, 1950).

Darrow, Clarence S. Debate and Lecture Pamphlets (debate opponent is indicated).

*Debate on the Theory of Non-Resistance to Evil* (n.d.) Arthur M.
Lewis.

*Marx versus Tolstoy* (1911) Arthur M. Lewis.

*Industrial Conspiracies* (1912) Lecture.

*The War in Europe* (1918) Lecture.

*War Prisoners* (1919) Lecture.

*Will Socialism Save the World?* (1919) John C. Kennedy.
*Debate on Capital Punishment* (1925) Judge Alfred J. Talley.
*Is the Human Race Getting Anywhere?* (1925) Frederick Starr.
*Is Life Worth Living?* (1925) Frederick Starr.
*Debate on Prohibition* (1925) John Haynes Holmes.
*Dry-Law Debate* (1927) Wayne B. Wheeler.
*Debate Concerning a General Purpose in the Universe* (1928) Alfred W. Wishart.
*The Open Shop: A Defense of Union Labor* (1929) Lecture.
*Is the U. S. Immigration Law Beneficial?* (1929) Lothrop Stoddard.
*Environment versus Heredity* (1930) Dr. Albert Edward Wiggam.
*Should the Eighteenth Amendment Be Repealed?* (1931) Clarence True Wilson.

Ghodes, Clarence. *The Periodicals of American Transcendentalism* (Durham, 1931). Chapter XVI deals with *The Index.*
Ginger, Ray. *Altgeld's America: The Lincoln Ideal versus Changing Realities* (New York, 1958). Thorough portrayal of early Darrow, his political development and his intellectual milieu.
——. *Six Days or Forever?: Tennessee v. John Thomas Scopes* (Boston, 1958). An acute analysis of the backgrounds and implications of the "Monkey Trial."
Goldman, Eric. *Rendezvous with Destiny: A History of Modern American Reform* (New York, 1952). Delineates perceptively the dichotomized Darwinians, Reform and Conservative.
Gronlund, Laurence. *The Cooperative Commonwealth in Its Outlines; An Exposition of Modern Socialism* (Boston & New York, 1884). Highly influential in its time.
Haldeman-Julius, Marcet. *Darrow's Two Great Trials* (Girard, 1927). An account of both the Leopold-Loeb "compulsion" murder case and the Sweet murder trial.
Harrison, Charles Yale. *Clarence Darrow* (New York, 1931).
Hoffman, Frederick T. *The Twenties: American Writing of the Postwar Decade* (New York, 1955). A brilliant reading of the literature and study of the times.
Kennedy, Gail (ed.) *Democracy and the Gospel of Wealth* (Boston, 1949). Essays by Andrew Carnegie, William Graham Sumner, Thorstein Veblen and others.

Kerr, Charles H. *A Socialist Publishing House* (Chicago, n.d.). A pamphlet outlining the history of Kerr's experiment in Utopian publication.

Knight, Grant C. *The Critical Period in American Literature* (Chapel Hill, 1951). American literature and thought of the 1890's intelligently analyzed and correlated with history.

——. *The Strenuous Age in American Literature* (Chapel Hill, 1954). Analysis of American intellectual patterns during the first decade of the twentieth century.

Kogan, Bernard R. (ed.). *The Chicago Haymarket Riot: Anarchy on Trial* (Boston, 1959). A reprinting of fugitive source documents relating to the entire background and proceedings of this unfortunate episode in American social history.

McLoughlin, William G. *Modern Revivalism* (New York, 1959).

Murray, Robert K. *Red Scare: A Study in National Hysteria, 1919–1920* (Minneapolis, 1955). Thoroughly documented account of frenzied Neo-Puritanism in America after World War I.

Nevins, Allan (ed.). *Letters and Journal of Brand Whitlock* (New York, 1936). Darrow is portrayed as a literary talent scout and a first-rate artist.

Parrington, Vernon L., Jr. *American Dreams: A Study of American Utopias* (Providence, 1947). Chapter XIII deals exclusively with The Charles H. Kerr Company of Chicago and its "stable" of Utopian writers.

Persons, Stow (ed.). *Evolutionary Thought in America* (New Haven, 1950).

——. *Free Religion: An American Faith* (New Haven, 1947). A full account of Francis Ellingwood Abbot and *The Index*.

Sherman, Stuart P. *Genius of America: Studies in Behalf of the Younger Generation* (New York, 1923). "What Is A Puritan?" (pp. 33–71) is a sympathetic, scholarly treatment opposed to Darrow's concept of this theological enigma.

Stone, Irving. *Clarence Darrow for the Defense* (New York, 1941). A popular account of the attorney's life and trials.

Sumner, William Graham. *What the Social Classes Owe to Each Other* (New York, 1883).

*Unity Magazine: In Memoriam, Clarence Darrow* (May 16, 1938). Essays by Harry Elmer Barnes, Arthur Garfield Hays, James

Weldon Johnson, and other friends and associates of the attorney.

Waller, George M. (ed.). *Puritanism in Early America* (Boston, 1950). Essays by Charles Francis Adams, Charles A. Beard, Samuel Eliot Morrison, Ralph Barton Perry, and other scholars.

Weinberg, Arthur (ed.) *Attorney for the Damned* (New York, 1957). A valuable collection of Darrow speeches and summations.

Weinberg, Arthur & Weinberg, Lila (eds.). *The Muckrakers* (New York, 1961).

# INDEX